£2

marlborough
wine

STORIES FROM NEW ZEALAND'S PREMIER WINE REGION

Photographs by Frank Gasteiger

Bernard
Sorry you can only
enjoy Marlborough
at a distance! But
hope you enjoy this
virtual tour.
Hazel.

ORIEL
Design & Publishing

WINE
MARLBOROUGH
NEW ZEALAND

Contents

Introduction

Nau mai, haere mai, welcome to Marlborough, whether you are actually here in New Zealand's premier wine region, or visiting us virtually by opening this book.

Remarkably, it is now just over three decades since Marlborough's first commercial vineyards were planted. In that time the wine industry has transformed the region visually, socially and economically. It has also taken us from relative obscurity to being recognised as a leading new world wine region.

For many of you, Marlborough will be synonymous with the wine style that put us firmly on the wine map in the early days – sauvignon blanc. We are thrilled that international wine critics continue to celebrate our sauvignon blanc, and marvel at what we have achieved in so short a time. But there is so much more to Marlborough than sauvignon blanc, and our reputation continues to grow and broaden, enhanced by our seductive pinot noir, superb chardonnay, and stunning aromatics.

Marlborough has a unique mix of climate, topography and soils, with sub-regions and micro-regions of infinite variety. Our success is undoubtedly the product of a partnership between this wonderful terroir and the people who work with it every day. Without the foresight, hard work, risk-taking, skill and dedication of our growers and winemakers, Marlborough would not have gained its enviable reputation or stayed ahead in a fiercely competitive international marketplace.

Many of our viticulturists and winemakers are born and bred New Zealanders, whilst others come from overseas, attracted by the wine growing environment, fresh thinking, opportunities for innovation, and of course, the Marlborough lifestyle. In the vineyards, a small army of seasonal workers, many of them from the Pacific Islands, play an important part in the industry, planting, pruning, plucking and picking. Ours is a vibrant, diverse and fascinating community, and this book introduces you to it through the stories of the wine companies and the personalities behind the wine labels.

The first book about Marlborough wine was Cynthia Brookes' Marlborough Wines & Vines, published in 1992. So much has happened since then, that it is time for a new look at what Marlborough wine is all about. I hope you enjoy touring the Marlborough wine region through these pages, and that the book inspires you to explore further by visiting cellar doors and viewing websites, and by sampling our wines here in Marlborough or wherever you are in the world.

Kia ora! Cheers!

Blair Gibbs
CHAIRMAN, WINE MARLBOROUGH

There is a place at the southern edge of the South Pacific where whales break the ocean surface within sight of land, and narrow valleys rise from a rugged coastline to sometimes snow-capped peaks. Here, grapevines carpet the valley floors and creep into the foothills.

The place is Marlborough, in the north east of New Zealand's South Island, a region of 17,500 square kilometres and a population of 44,000.

Marlborough Wine

Today Marlborough is New Zealand's most planted wine region. In the span of just a few decades the wines of this small yet geographically diverse region have risen to prominence and attracted the kind of international acclaim more usually afforded the wines of the long-established wine regions of the old world.

Inspired by the infinite nuances of flavour offered by Marlborough's climate, soils and landscape, the region's wine repertoire continues to expand. Marlborough is now well known, not only for its flagship variety, sauvignon blanc, but also for its chardonnay, sparkling wines, riesling, pinot gris, gewürztraminer and increasingly, for its pinot noir. These are stylish wines with pure, intense flavours, wonderful aromas and stunning vibrancy. They surprise and delight and each one embodies the signature of this very special place.

Marlborough is a region of spectacular natural beauty and remarkable bounty. In past centuries, Māori hunted moa here and cultivated vast kumara crops in the year-round sunshine. The ocean to the east, and the waterways of the Marlborough Sounds to the north, have always provided all manner of seafood. On the fertile rolling downs of the river valleys, early European settlers established the country's pastoral industry and planted extensive orchards.

In 1973, Marlborough's first large scale, modern vineyard was planted by the Montana company after the region's potential had been spotted by Ivan Yukich, one of the pioneers of the New Zealand wine industry we know today. But Montana's was not the first wine to be made from the fruit of Marlborough vines. The first vineyards had been planted a century earlier.

The early winemakers

In 1873, Scottish farmer David Herd started a wine venture on land known as Auntsfield, at the end of Paynters Road in what is now defined as the Southern Valleys sub-region. Herd planted less than half a hectare in what were probably red muscatel vines and used a vine trellis system similar to that used to this day. The grapes were crushed with wheels from the local flax mill and the wine, fermented with baker's yeast and brown sugar, was matured in used brandy barrels. The original wine cellar is pictured above. Later run by his brother-in-law Bill Paynter, Herd's vineyard continued to produce grapes for wine until 1931.

Another wine business was established in 1880 at Mount Pleasant, Koromiko, between Blenheim and Picton. Here the Freeth family had a vineyard and bought grapes from other growers in the area to make sherry, madeira, port and constancia. Until 1958 the Freeth Brothers winery supplied customers throughout the country.

Over a similar period, the Peters family, originally from Lebanon, were making wine from grapes grown around their Blenheim property. In the 1890s Mansoor Peters obtained a licence to make and sell wines which included sherry and port tonic wine. From their Main Street general store and a travelling store, the family sold wines to hotels, restaurants and private buyers across the top of the South Island. The family made wine until the 1960s.

There are records of other small vineyard enterprises including a vineyard planted by Italian immigrants in the Outer Sounds after World War I and the first vineyard in the Waihopai Valley, planted in 1972. A new permanent exhibition at the Marlborough Museum will add more detail to the stories of these early pioneers, through a collection of artefacts including a huge variety of wines, vineyard and winery equipment, tools, documents, photographs, anecdotes and interactive displays.

Modern pioneers

In August 1973 the first vines of the modern era of grape growing in Marlborough were planted. When local farmers saw what Montana was doing, committing huge resources to converting sheep and arable farmland to vineyards, they too began to discuss and explore the potential for growing grapes.

Trial and error might best describe the process by which the growers and winemakers of the late 1970s made the transition to their new industry, but their knowledge of Marlborough, its climate and its soils, meant that it was not long before spectacular results were being achieved. The challenges of the region's diverse conditions demanded resourceful viticulture and an unrelenting dedication to the task

of making premium wine. Pioneering spirit, adaptability and passion underpin Marlborough's extraordinary success.

Many of those early pioneers are still leaders in the Marlborough wine world. The tradition of daughters and sons joining the family farming business is unbroken and new generations, who have been brought up in a Marlborough very different to the Marlborough of their parent's youth, are helping to take the industry forward.

At the same time, new blood has come into Marlborough with Switzerland, the Netherlands, the United Kindgom, Belgium, France, Germany, Portugal, the USA, Reunion, Australia and all parts of New Zealand represented amongst the region's growers and winemakers. The international dimension adds to the strength of Marlborough's wine community and brings a rich diversity to the region's wines and culture.

For those just entering the industry or wanting to develop their careers, degrees in oenology and winemaking are offered by New Zealand universities. These are supported by study opportunities at the Nelson Marlborough Institute of Technology and research programmes at the Marlborough Wine Research Centre based in Blenheim.

Much viticulture training is on-the-job, and awards such as the Silver Secateurs and Young Viticulturist of the Year recognise and celebrate exceptional skills.

Marlborough vineyards now cover over 22,000 hectares and as the area increases, so too does the amount of vine management work. Thousands of vineyard workers are needed to do the essential tasks of grafting, pruning, thinning, leaf plucking and hand picking. Demand for labour now far outstrips domestic supply, so overseas workers are employed on a seasonal basis, many coming from the Pacific Islands. These men and women, who swap tropical climates for Marlborough's chilly and often damp winters, are also pioneers. They face the challenges of an unfamiliar culture in a foreign land. Most will never have seen a vineyard before their first season in Marlborough, but they quickly learn new skills and many return, making a vital contribution to the successful expansion of the region's wine industry.

Unique terroir

As any winemaker will tell you, the best wines are created, first and foremost, in the vineyard; by which they mean that success is as much to do with everything that happens before harvesting as it is to do with what happens later. Of course the handling of the harvested fruit, blending, fermentation and ageing all have a part to play but arguably the most important characteristics are created by the magical synergy of climate, landscape and soil found in a region, a sub-region, a micro-region or even a single vineyard. This combination is known in the wine world as the

terroir. The uniqueness of a particular terroir is something every winemaker wants to express in their wines.

Sunny days, cool nights and free-draining soils

Marlborough is one of New Zealand's sunniest regions with around 2,500 sunshine hours a year, and one of the driest with an average annual rainfall of 647mm. Positioned at 41.3 degrees south, a mid-point on the world's wine belt, Marlborough shares its latitude with many long-established wine regions. But its proximity to the Pacific Ocean, prevailing winds and isolation from continental hot air masses, creates a temperate maritime climate with much cooler summers and milder winters than those experienced in its northern hemisphere latitudinal equivalents.

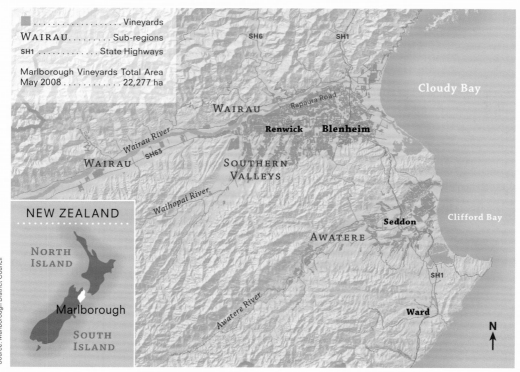

Source: Marlborough District Council

Marlborough's summer heat is tempered by cooling easterly sea breezes and extended, mild, dry autumns providing ideal conditions for long slow ripening of grapes prior to vintage.

This 'cool viticultural climate' is characteristic of the upper Loire Valley, Champagne and northern Burgundy in France, but in Marlborough the effect is magnified by the significant difference in temperature between day and night – commonly 10°C in summer. This extreme diurnal variation slows development of sugars, preserves the natural acidity in the grapes and gives rise to the intense varietal characters and succulent ripe fruit flavours for which Marlborough wines are renowned.

Whilst climate is crucial to the character of Marlborough wine, so too is the soil in which the grapes are grown. Compared to the terrain of the old world wine regions, Marlborough's is a very young landform. Myriad soil types have resulted from the effects of climate conditions including glacial activity. Rivers of melt-water carried glacial debris down from the mountains and out onto the broad alluvial plains.

Marlborough's landscape, favourable climate, desirable free-draining soils, pure rivers and natural aquifers together provide the ideal environment for the creation of exquisite wines.

Infinite variety

Soil variations, coupled with differences in topography, aspect, rainfall and temperature, give rise to viticultural sub-regions each characterised by distinct growing conditions that are reflected in quite different wines.

Winemakers sometimes take fruit from two or more sub-regions, combining their juices to create complexity in the wines. However there is an increasing interest in capturing the flavour characteristics of a particular place, expressing its unique terroir.

Marlborough wines are increasingly being defined in terms of sub-regions by their makers and by commentators. Wairau, Southern Valleys and Awatere are the three most obvious sub-regions with a fourth, Kaikoura, covering the recent development of vineyards south of Ward.

SUB-REGION	TEMPERATURE	MOISTURE	TYPICAL SOIL TYPE
Wairau			
Including Rapaura, Lower Wairau, Conders Bend, Renwick and Kaituna	Cool	Dry	River flood plain – extremely variable soils, from stony river wash to fine, deep alluvium seams.
Southern Valleys			
Including Ben Morven, Brancott, Fairhall, Omaka and Waihopai	Cooler	Drier	Glacial outwash – older variable soils exhibiting stony gravels with higher levels of clay.
Awatere			
Including Seaview, Redwood Pass and Blind River	Coolest	Driest	River terraces and flood plains – alluvial gravels and clay with wind blown loess.

These sub-regions are in turn divided into smaller sub-regions – individual valleys and areas that growers and winemakers identify as having unique conditions; for example Rapaura, Brancott, Renwick and Blind River.

Wairau

This sub-region is defined by the Wairau Valley through which runs a river flowing from the mountains in the west to the ocean at Cloudy Bay.

Wairau is a Māori word meaning 'many waters' referring to the river's braided form which spreads across a wide alluvial plain. Marlborough's earliest vineyards were established in this valley which includes the acclaimed Rapaura and Renwick areas, home to some of the region's pioneer wine companies and best known wines.

Southern Valleys

The Southern Valleys sub-region comprises those valleys that lie to the south of the Wairau plain. Each valley's river is a tributary of the Wairau River. The soils of the Ben Morven, Brancott, Omaka, Fairhall and Waihopai Valleys typically originate from glacial outwash and tend to have significant amounts of gravel and higher levels of clay than the other sub-regions.

Cold air descending from the nearby mountains creates a cooler, later ripening climate than that of the growing areas on the opposite, northern side of the Wairau plain.

Awatere

This sub-region, south east of the Wairau Valley, comprises the Awatere River valley, Seaview, Redwood Pass and Blind River areas.

The Māori word *Awatere* means 'fast flowing stream'. The soils here are typically stony with alluvial gravel on wind borne loess. More exposed to cold weather from the south than the other sub-regions, the Awatere has a longer growing season and slower ripening conditions.

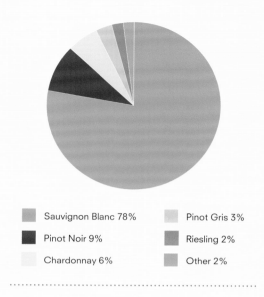

Sauvignon Blanc 78%	Pinot Gris 3%
Pinot Noir 9%	Riesling 2%
Chardonnay 6%	Other 2%

Marlborough Wine Styles

Marlborough sauvignon blanc is widely acclaimed as the modern pinnacle of the variety. In only a few other places, including in its French homeland, is sauvignon blanc quite so distinctive, so breathtaking in its flavour and aroma. There is no doubt that sauvignon blanc put Marlborough on the world wine map and brought the region to the attention of serious wine drinkers everywhere.

But the region has not rested on its laurels. Motivated by their achievements with sauvignon blanc, Marlborough's wine companies have gone on to identify other varieties suited to the region's unique terroir. Chardonnay and aromatic wines, like riesling, pinot gris and gewürztraminer, have always been represented in small quantities but more vineyards are now being planted in these varieties in response to a marketplace that acknowledges Marlborough's suitability for producing world class examples. Regardless of this, the fastest rising star is pinot noir. Marlborough is taking full advantage of being one of the few places in the world where all the conditions required to grow this variety are present. Pinot noir already accounts for around

9% of annual production and its importance is likely to increase in the next few years.

Sauvignon Blanc

In August 1973 Montana planted their first vines in Marlborough – sauvignon blanc cuttings from vines grown in the Auckland region. Before very long, Marlborough sauvignon blanc was taking the world by storm, winning awards and being noticed by critics and consumers alike. In his 2002 New Wine Atlas, the wine writer Oz Clarke described the initial impact of Marlborough sauvignon blanc, "No previous wine had shocked, thrilled, offended, entranced the world before with such brash, unexpected flavours of gooseberries, passion fruit and lime, or crunchy green capsicums and asparagus spears."

Enthusiasm for Marlborough sauvignon blanc continues unabated and, although Marlborough's growers have successfully introduced other varieties, sauvignon blanc is still by far the region's most planted variety, accounting for over three quarters of total production.

The majority of sauvignon blanc is cold fermented in stainless steel tanks, but the winemaker's masterstroke is in the use of other techniques such as fermenting or ageing small portions in mostly older oak, or maturing components on yeast lees for a fuller, richer style. By combining fruit from vineyard parcels that have different characteristics, wines with Marlborough's distinctive signature result.

Vibrant, pungent, fresh, zesty and herbaceous are common descriptors of Marlborough's sauvignon blanc. So it comes as no surprise that this wine goes perfectly with Marlborough's fresh produce and the al fresco, casual but sophisticated cuisine that the region's vineyard restaurants do so well.

Pinot Noir

This ancient red variety was first planted in New Zealand in the 1970s. Marlborough is ideally suited to growing pinot noir which enjoys cool temperatures, low rainfall and the soil types found in this region. Unlike white wine grapes, pinot noir grapes are cold soaked before fermentation and then gently macerated and plunged during fermentation to extract fine aromas, elegant tannins and just the right colour from the thin red skins of the pinot noir berries.

Pinot noir goes wonderfully with meats, winter vegetables and pasta dishes. In Marlborough, try it with local wild game like venison, pork, rabbit and goat, or with lamb or beef.

Chardonnay

Chardonnay is Marlborough's third most planted grape variety. Premium chardonnays are made from hand picked fruit which is whole-bunch pressed and fermented in French oak barrels. The flavour profile of chardonnay varies considerably depending on winemaker influence, from rich and mellow with lovely grapefruit and butterscotch notes through to lighter and even unoaked interpretations. Chardonnay is versatile and goes well with all but the most delicate of savoury or sweet dishes. In Marlborough, try it with local fish, shellfish, crayfish, with pasta or white meats, or with a simple, long, lazy lunch of breads, cheese and Marlborough olive oil.

Riesling, Pinot Gris and Gewürztraminer

Riesling, pinot gris and gewürztraminer are aromatic varieties characterised by their distinctive aromas and flavours, ranging from dry and flinty to rich and fruity. In the winery, the grapes are pressed to remove the skins with the juice fermented at very cool temperatures in stainless steel tanks.

Sweet, dessert wines are sometimes made from these varieties by leaving grapes on the vine at the end of the harvest until they are affected by a botrytis mould, often referred to as 'noble rot'.

Dry aromatic wines go well with summer foods, salads, fish and chicken, while the sweeter aromatics are gaining popularity as good matches for spicy foods including Asian dishes, shellfish and sharp cheese. Luscious dessert wines are to be enjoyed at the end of a meal with delicious sweet things.

Sparkling Wine

Marlborough's sparkling wines are usually made from chardonnay and pinot noir grapes using traditional techniques. Some Marlborough producers of sparkling wine have long-standing ties with French Champagne makers, and these collaborations have resulted in distinctive Marlborough wines that also have the quality characteristics of their Champagne ancestors.

Grapes for sparkling wine are picked at an early stage of ripeness to retain fruit aroma and flavour along with delicate and firm acid, this being on average some three weeks earlier than mature ripeness for table wines. The fruit is traditionally hand picked and after fermentation, the juice is blended to produce the expected delicate flavour and soft texture of a sparkling wine. The wines undergo a second fermentation and a long period of maturation in the bottle, periodically turned fractionally, known as riddling. At between 18 months and four or more years old, the wine is ready to enjoy, particularly with everything the sea has to offer and other fine foods, or as an aperitif.

Looking after the environment

Wine quality is inextricably linked to the quality of the environment in which the grapes are grown and there is a high level of awareness about the need to care for the elements that support the wine industry in Marlborough.

Marlborough is well represented in the Sustainable Winegrowing New Zealand programme, which encourages the use of environmentally responsible management in the vineyard and in the winery. SWNZ provides advice and sets standards against which wine companies can be assessed to achieve accreditation.

To remove the need for netting and bird scaring contraptions, a number of growers are working to reintroduce the kārearea, or New Zealand falcon, and they are having some success. This virtually extinct bird, a remarkably agile but delicate creature, was once commonly found throughout the region. It is fairly certain that grapes will not be damaged by other pest species when a karearea is patrolling the skies.

Carbon neutrality is a hot topic and some wine companies have achieved, or are aiming for, carbon neutrality under the Landcare Research carboNZero® accreditation scheme. The scheme helps wine companies measure, reduce and offset carbon emissions.

Organic and biodynamic vineyard and production practices are becoming more popular, with many wine companies working to minimise the use of synthetic chemicals in the growing process and increasing their use of environmentally safe technologies. For some companies the philosophy is central to their whole approach to winemaking and these provide inspiration and valuable encouragement to others.

At the Marlborough Wine Research Centre, the organisation works to support the wine industry through the study of such topics as the influence of climate on fruit characteristics,

pest and disease management, yield prediction, sustainable production and much more. One of the Centre's projects is trying to describe the flavour of Marlborough sauvignon blanc, not in the words of a wine critic, but with scientific precision, and to understand the wine's flavour characteristics from a psychological point of view. This is groundbreaking work.

From strength to strength

Unique growing conditions, the blending of 21st century science with the ancient arts of grape growing and winemaking, people with stamina and passion, forward thinking businesses, innovation and enterprise; all these things have contributed to forging Marlborough's reputation as a wine region and will continue to feature in the story of Marlborough wine that has yet to unfold. This book captures and celebrates the story so far and offers a preview of what the future might have in store.

The Marlborough wine year

Month	Vineyard	Winery
January	Leaf plucking.	Preparation for vintage. Training cellar staff.
February	Veraison (the beginning of ripening). Fruit sampling.	Analysing fruit samples.
March	Fruit sampling. Harvest planning. Harvesting.	Processing grapes.
April	Harvesting.	Processing grapes.
May	Autumn colours in the vineyard.	Winemaking.
June	Pruning.	Winemaking.
July	Pruning and mulching.	Blending and bottling whites.
August	Pruning. Replanting if required.	Bottling whites. Ageing reds.
September	Final last minute pruning. Leaves starting to grow.	Possible vintage overseas for winemaker experience. Marketing overseas.
October	Bud burst. Shoot thinning.	Marketing overseas.
November	Canopy management.	Marketing overseas. Winery maintenance.
December	Shoot thinning. Bud rubbing.	Rest before another vintage.

Stories of Marlborough winemakers

The stories in the following pages will introduce you to the companies and personalities behind the wine labels and take you on a fascinating tour of the Marlborough wine region.

Finding out more about the wines and their makers

A panel accompanying each story provides the practical information you need to explore further by viewing the company's website, visiting the cellar door if there is one, or making contact with the company to find out more about the wines and where to buy them.

Visiting the cellar doors

Cellar door is the term used in New Zealand to refer to a tasting room where you can sample and purchase wines. Not all wine companies have cellar doors. Some cellar doors offer light food or have cafés or restaurants attached and some have other attractions, for example gardens or an art exhibition. You can sometimes take a tour of the vineyard or winery.

Wine Trail Map

Inside the back cover of the book you will find a wine trail map which provides information about cellar doors that are open to the public. Before you set off for a cellar door, check the opening times. In some cases you will need to make an appointment.

Though it is not yet where she lives, Rebecca Salmond clearly feels at home on her 27.5 hectares in the Brancott Valley, at the foot of the Wrekin Hills. Striding confidently up the steep incline, past the rows of vines planted since 2000, she explains her plans, pointing out where new terracing will happen and where she will one day build her winery next to the little dam where she teaches her children to sail.

A continuing journey

Eventually we reach the top and marvel at the rock sculptures, huge faces surveying the view from Cook Strait to way out west down the Wairau Valley and across to the Richmond Range. When the vineyard was first being developed, a family friend, Samoan artist Fatu Feu'u, spent a summer here and Rebecca feels that his works imbue the place with a spirit, a sense of rightness and groundedness that will eventually pull her, and her family, here to live permanently.

But for now, Rebecca continues the nomadic life she started when she left New Zealand to study winemaking at Roseworthy College in South Australia. From there she travelled the globe, as she puts it, "on the smell of an oily rag and the meager wages of a rookie winemaker." Eventually returning to New Zealand, she and brother Simon came across this property and despite its inauspicious position believed that it would be perfect for pinot noir. Rebecca had seen grapes grown in all sorts of places and was sure that a European approach to vineyard design and management would work. She has been proved right.

"I have immense appreciation and respect for the old world wine styles and winemakers who balance art and science so that the wine is truly an expression of the terroir, the region and producer.

I aim to make these true wines from our Marlborough vineyard, where the vines are meticulously managed to produce the style of wine we are after. Just subtle changes are then made to the wine in the tank. We use fine grain French

oak, but sparingly. Subtlety and elegance are what I am trying to achieve, and the wines must go with food. We're not only producing wonderful pinot noir from these silt loam soils but also excellent sauvignon blanc and pinot gris."

Between vintages Rebecca still travels, now with her partner, who works for New Zealand's Americas Cup team, and their two children. Her vineyard manager looks after things in Marlborough and wherever she is, Rebecca is running the business from her laptop. "But now we're looking forward to coming home to Marlborough and I'm excited about where Odyssey will take me and where I can take Odyssey from here."

Odyssey Wines

www.odysseywines.co.nz
PO Box 21655, Henderson,
Waitakere 0650
T + 64 9 837 5410
sales@odysseywines.co.nz

Owned by
Rebecca Salmond

Brands
Odyssey, Homer, Behave

Varieties
Sauvignon Blanc, Pinot Gris, Pinot Noir

Sub-region
Southern Valleys

Family affair

Whether it is sheep and deer in Canterbury, or sheep and crops in Southland, farming is a hard business. Growing grapes in Marlborough isn't easy either, but for the Smalls and the Smiths it beats being out in all weathers and the vagaries of dealing with livestock.

The Smalls are Ken and Jill who planted the first vines on their Brancott Valley property in 1982. The Smiths, Julie and Stuart, joined in 1994 and Fairhall Downs was born. Julie is Ken and Jill's daughter. Three Smith children are already helping out in the school holidays. So, like so many wine companies, this is a family business.

The Brancott is one of Marlborough's Southern Valleys, higher, at 90 metres above sea level, than the Wairau plain, and with much older soils. At Fairhall Downs they say those differences can be picked up in the texture and long finish of the wines; four varieties, sauvignon blanc, chardonnay, pinot gris and pinot noir.

The vineyard is run strictly to sustainable principles, which means that the aim is to leave the land in the same or an even better state than they found it, so that future generations can benefit from what it has to offer. The theory is simple, "Allow the wines to show their sense of place or their terroir without interfering too much." Of course, the practice is a bit more tricky than the theory makes it sound, and it takes dedication and tenacity to make sure the business

The vineyard is run strictly to sustainable principles ... the aim is to leave the land in the same or an even better state than they found it.

sticks firmly to its own rules, learning how to do things better at every turn.

Jill sums up the Fairhall Downs philosophy, "Our wines get noticed by people who love wine and enjoy the differences between varietals and regions and brands. We are growing our grapes and making our wines with those people in mind. Why wouldn't we do our best? Doing anything less would not be challenging enough for this family!"

Fairhall Downs

www.fairhalldowns.co.nz

70 Wrekin Road,
RD2, Blenheim 7272
T + 64 3 572 8356
sales@fairhalldowns.co.nz

Owned by
Stuart Smith & Ken Small

Brand
Fairhall Downs

Varieties
Sauvignon Blanc, Pinot Gris,
Chardonnay, Pinot Noir

Sub-region
Southern Valleys

SWNZ accredited vineyard(s)

Visit
70 Wrekin Road,
off Brancott Road,
Blenheim

• Cellar door

• Vineyard tours by
arrangement

• Wedding venue

A philosophy of give and take

Frogs are a sign of a healthy environment and the southern bell frog, found in the restored wetlands around Grove Mill winery and as the logo on the company's wine label, signifies the importance of the environment to this innovative wine business.

"Sustainability is a word that is used too loosely," says Rob White, Grove Mill CEO, "but for us it means living by our values, resulting in a win-win situation for everyone. Balancing what we take and what we give, actually makes good business sense as well as being environmentally responsible." "And it makes great wine as well," adds chief winemaker Dave Pearce.

Viticulturist Doug Holmes and his team have a tough job, monitoring and managing the grapes across 15 vineyards to ensure that full advantage is taken of the variety of soils and climate conditions, and that each block delivers exactly the characteristics being sought by the winemakers.

Grove Mill's range includes chardonnay, pinot gris, pinot noir, riesling and of course, sauvignon blanc. Production has reached 70,000 cases. The business occupies a striking architect-designed building in the Wairau Valley set between the vines of the home vineyard and the wetland sanctuary.

Rob White enjoys watching Grove Mill's reputation grow on the basis of quality, both in terms of the finished product and the way the wines are produced. "Our vineyards are our future. To be proud to present our wines to the world, we need to take care of our world. We are trying to make this a habit not a hardship, and we're getting there."

Grove Mill
....
www.grovemill.co.nz

PO Box 67, Renwick 7243
T + 64 3 572 8200
info@nzwineco.co.nz

Owned by
The New Zealand
Wine Company

Brands
Grove Mill, Sanctuary, Frog Haven
Varieties Sauvignon Blanc,
Pinot Noir, Riesling, Pinot Gris
Chardonnay, Gewürztraminer
Sub-regions
Wairau, Southern Valleys

SWNZ accredited vineyard(s)
SWNZ accredited winery
Certified carboNZero®

Visit
Corner State Highway 63
& Waihopai Valley Road,
Renwick
• Cellar door
• Vine Library
• Aroma Demonstration
• The Diversion Art
  Gallery
• Wetland
• Picnic area

Fine dining for vines

In 1989 two wind-surfing mates, restaurateur Chris Gambitsis and police detective Phil Binnie, decided that enjoying wine was not enough and what they really wanted to do was grow grapes and make their own wine.

In true Kiwi fashion they jumped in the deep end and set about establishing the Falcon Vineyard on a notoriously stony stretch of the Wairau river valley. They named their fledgling operation Lake Chalice Wines after the wilderness lake in the Richmond Range and adopted the karearea, the New Zealand falcon, as their emblem.

The falcon is an awesome predator taking prey up to six times its own weight, fearlessly protecting its nest and young, capable of pulling 17 g-force in the turn, and of diving at speeds of up to 320 kph. Lake Chalice wines is a sponsor of the Wingspan Trust which works to preserve New Zealand's birds of prey, and is active in Falcons for Grapes, a project attempting to re-establish falcons in the Wairau Valley.

Chris and Phil are keen sportsmen and firmly believe that like humans, vines need the right diet if they are going to be high performers. When they were offered a load of seaweed they snapped it up as a treat for their pinot noir vines. "A feed of seaweed gives them nitrogen, potassium, phosphorus and a myriad of other trace elements and minerals," says Phil. Natural mulches, fertiliser courtesy of a flock of sheep and compost made with grape marc are just some of the other menu items that go to nourish Lake Chalice's sauvignon blanc, pinot noir, riesling, chardonnay, pinot gris and merlot vines.

"Our wines have a name for consistently high quality and we'll always strive to keep that reputation," says Chris whose background in restaurants gives him a keen appreciation of what wine buyers value. "If it isn't a wine I'd be proud to serve to my most discerning diner," says Chris, "it's not a Lake Chalice wine."

Lake Chalice Wines

....

www.lakechalice.com

PO Box 66, Renwick 7243
T + 64 3 572 9327
wine@lakechalice.com

Owned by Phil Binnie & Christopher Gambitsis

Brands
Lake Chalice, Platinum, Raptor

Varieties Sauvignon Blanc, Pinot Noir, Pinot Gris, Riesling, Chardonnay, Merlot

Sub-regions Wairau, Awatere, Southern Valleys

SWNZ accredited vineyard(s)

Visit
93 Vintage Lane, Renwick

• Cellar door

Māori wine pioneers making their mark

"**Y**ou can sum up the way Māori feel about their relationship with the land and the sea in one word – *kaitiakitanga* – guardianship," says James Wheeler, brand ambassador of Tohu Wines, the first Māori owned commercial wine exporting company. "The land and the sea are the givers of life. The wine we make is our gift from the land – *ngā hua a te whenua*. We believe we all have a responsibility to look after what we have been given so that it continues to provide for us and those who come after us."

In keeping with the Māori practice of holding property collectively for the common good rather than individually for private gain, the Tohu company is owned by thousands of Māori through Wakatū Incorporation, Wī Pere Trust and Ngāti Rārua Ātiawa Iwi Trust.

Henry Beauchamp (right) is responsible for Tohu's Awatere vineyard which covers 71 hectares producing sauvignon blanc, pinot noir and riesling grapes. He is a pioneer in that when he started there were very few Māori involved in viticulture. But he is a man of the land. He understands the weather and all about persuading the soil to produce its best.

"We produce wine with respect for the earth mother, Papatūanuku, and our ancestors who have preserved this land for our current generation. Sustainability is central to everything we do; not damaging the land and not contributing to climate change."

Tohu, which translates into English as 'signature', is rapidly gaining a worldwide reputation for producing top quality wines in accordance with Māori traditions of spirituality and harmony with nature. Since the first vintage in 1998, the Tohu approach has been paying off handsomely with steady increases in volume and

range and new markets being opened up all the time. The Tohu vision of achievement through respect for people and place is being achieved. As Māori would say, *Manaaki whenua, manaaki tangata, haere whakamua* – Care for the land, care for the people, go forward.

"We produce wine with respect for the earth mother, Papatūanuku, and our ancestors who have preserved this land for our current generation. Sustainability is central to everything we do."

Tohu Wines
....
www.tohuwines.co.nz

PO Box 1028, Blenheim 7240
T + 64 3 520 9230
enquiries@tohu.co.nz

Owned by Wakatū Incorporation, Wi Pere Trust, Ngāti Rārua Ātiawa Iwi Trust

Brand Tohu

Varieties Sauvignon Blanc, Pinot Gris, Chardonnay, Riesling, Pinot Noir, Merlot

Sub-regions
Awatere, Southern Valleys

SWNZ accredited vineyard(s)

Visit
The Wine Room, SH1, 3kms north of Blenheim

• Cellar door
• Café

A formidable team

Dog Point headquarters is a scene of telling contrasts. On one side of the yard, shaded by a stand of birch trees, sits a wonderfully quaint corrugated iron woolshed. In the old sheep yards a flock of romneys and perendales graze the long grass, waiting for their turn amongst the vines. It's their job to mow between the rows, spreading their natural fertiliser as they go.

In contrast, on the other side of the yard is the sleek modern winery building, basic in all respects, but efficient and big enough to house all the barrels and tanks that you need for 21st century wine making. The design of the office building alongside mimics that of yesteryear and it sits snug in its corner, its verandah offering shelter to a line-up of gumboots and coats, and the dogs that come to work for exercise. But this building is wired to the world, and houses the lab and the meeting-tasting room. This is the engine room of a very modern business.

The links between the two sides of the yard are the people who run Dog Point, the Sutherlands and the Healys, now amongst the most experienced and respected of Marlborough's wine producers.

Ivan and Margaret Sutherland (far right) purchased land and planted grapes in the late 1970s, knowing that their vines would be nicely aged by the time they got around to founding their own label. Ivan planted pinot noir alongside the sauvignon blanc, gambling on pinot noir becoming a big thing for Marlborough one day. On all accounts he has been proven right.

In the late 1980s, Ivan was the viticulturist for Cloudy Bay and James Healy joined the company as an oenologist in 1991. The two found that they made a great team, a strong partnership that has endured. So when Ivan's maturing vines would wait no longer, they decided to start their own label. In 2002 Ivan and Margaret, and James and his wife Wendy (near right) established Dog Point, sourcing fruit from Estate owned valley and hillside vineyards on the southern side of the Wairau Valley. Old fashioned values prevail at every step of the process; low cropping, hand picking, hand sorting, wild yeast and oak barrel fermenting and ageing.

With a shared vision and a wealth of experience behind it, the label has quickly become established and it is no surprise that Dog Point wines are consistently commanding the very favourable attention of wine buyers both internationally and at home in New Zealand.

It has been said that "These boys know their stuff." Though calling them boys might be stretching it a little these days, the sentiment can't be disputed; they are a formidable team.

Dog Point

www.dogpoint.co.nz

PO Box 52, Renwick 7243
T + 64 3 572 8294
info@dogpoint.co.nz

Owned by
Ivan & Margaret Sutherland,
James & Wendy Healy

Brand Dog Point Vineyard

Varieties Sauvignon Blanc, Chardonnay, Pinot Noir

Sub-region Southern Valleys

SWNZ accredited vineyard(s)

Visit by appointment only

With a shared vision and a wealth of experience behind it, the label has quickly become established.

Never enough hours

Allan Scott is a name to conjure with in Marlborough. Some say Allan (above centre) is the most experienced grape grower in the region and after over 35 years growing, and nearly 20 making wine, he is certainly treated as an elder statesman of the industry. Everyone turns to him for advice. On a day off at home someone he has never heard of phones to ask what to do to keep the birds off the ripening fruit. "Put nets on," says Allan. "Can't afford it," says the caller. "Then maybe you shouldn't be growing grapes," says Allan, being practical but grinning broadly as he remembers that he was a novice once. "Sometimes I feel like saying, go find out for yourself just like I had to do, but I try to be kinder than that."

Allan may have his name on the label but this is truly a family venture. Allan and his wife Catherine have always been partners in the business right from the purchase of their first

The Scott family are doers. They believe in working hard but enjoying life to the full.

block of Marlborough land in 1975. As their children have grown they have found their own niches in the business. The Scott family are doers. They believe in working hard but enjoying life to the full. They are competitive, between themselves, in business and in sport.

Son Josh (above left) is definitely a chip off the old block. As if being the chief winemaker isn't a big enough job, he moonlights at his own boutique brewery across the road, creating some wonderfully unusual beers. Daughter Sara (above right) works as a viticulturist and is also involved in marketing Allan Scott wines worldwide, as is daughter Victoria.

The younger generation are mad keen outdoor types, their names appearing early on the finishers lists for the top endurance races as well as cycling events. Meanwhile father and mother keep saying they will slow down on the wine business and do more of the other things in life they would like to get to. But it's not that easy when you are still so driven, never quite satisfied, always improving things.

in the day

Four vineyards, each with its own characteristics, are planted in sauvignon blanc, riesling, pinot gris, gewürztraminer, chardonnay and pinot noir grapes. The drive is for ever more sustainable viticulture practices with the aim of becoming totally organic over time. For the business as a whole, a zero carbon footprint is the target. "There's always another idea to pursue," says Catherine, who over nearly two decades has developed the Scott's vineyard restaurant from a tasting room sideline to a destination in its own right and somewhere the wines can be shown off, matched with cuisine featuring fresh local produce.

Perhaps a time will come when Allan Scott will spend a whole day without thinking about grape growing and wine. But why change the habits of half a lifetime? All the signs are that that day is a long way off.

ALLAN
SCOTT
FAMILY WINEMAKERS

Allan Scott Family Winemakers
....
www.allanscott.com
Jackson's Road,
RD3, Blenheim 7273
T +64 3 572 9054
info@allanscott.co.nz
Owned by Allan Scott Wines & Estates Ltd.

Brand
Allan Scott

Varieties
Sauvignon Blanc, Riesling, Chardonnay, Pinot Gris, Gewürztraminer, Pinot Noir

Sub-region Wairau

SWNZ accredited vineyard(s)

Visit
Jackson's Road
Blenheim
- Cellar door
- Twelve Trees Vineyard Restaurant
- Gardens
- Winery tours by arrangement

In the footsteps
of a true pioneer

The roots of Auntsfield vines reach deep into the past. This is where Marlborough wine began. The clouds of dust stirred by passing columns of colonial troops and Māori war parties crossing the Wairau Plains had only recently settled when David Herd laid down the region's first commercial vines in 1873. They were the mother vines that launched what is now New Zealand's most significant wine region.

Today, the Cowley family is the new bunch on the old vine of Auntsfield. Brothers Ben (far right) and Luc (near right) are viticulturist

"Our job is to truly understand, master and express the authenticity, the uniqueness of this place."

and winemaker respectively. They are creating wines that are making their mark worldwide. But however successful they are, the Cowleys are determined to avoid the familiar trap of over-commercialisation and will remain satisfied with what they have. "Our job is to truly understand, master and express the authenticity, the uniqueness of this place," Ben says. "We'll only produce wines from the vines of Auntsfield, same as in the 1870s."

Ben and Luc's parents, Graeme and Linda, purchased Auntsfield in 1998 and together the family carried out detailed site surveys which led them to divide the estate into 40 separate blocks defined by individual soil type, aspect, row orientation, gradient, altitude, geology and hydrology. To this patchwork of fields and their fruit, Ben and Luc apply craftsmanship, science, art, love, blood, sweat and tears to achieve the results they want.

The pinot noir, for example, is drawn from over 20 different blocks, each free to develop its own style. The resulting wine is blended together late in the winemaking process. "By keeping each batch of wine separate until the very end, you create layers, not a singularity," says Luc. "It's like designing a good meal. You need complexity and texture, complementary flavours, the right spice with the right meat. Palate is the key issue."

Ben and Luc's commitment to low cropping, hand harvesting, barrel fermentation, lees stirring, indigenous yeast and all the nuances, innovations and eccentricities that true artisans bring to the process of creating chardonnay, sauvignon blanc and pinot noir, create wines that Luc describes as, "Complex and multi-layered,

with excellent concentration and length."

And taste doesn't get much longer than the Auntsfield Heritage Pinot Noir because it is infused with the contents of a bottle of David Herd's final vintage. The descendants of Marlborough wine's founding father generously gifted a bottle that had remained in the family since his death in 1905.

Adding the antique wine to the Heritage speaks volumes about the Cowleys and their dedication to expressing the unique character of the land where it all began. Anyone with a taste for history and a love of wine will savour every drop.

Auntsfield Estate

www.auntsfield.co.nz
270 Paynters Road,
RD2, Blenheim 7272
T + 64 3 578 0622
info@auntsfield.co.nz
Owned by
The Cowley Family

Brand Auntsfield Estate

Varieties Pinot Noir,
Chardonnay, Sauvignon Blanc

Sub-region Southern Valleys

SWNZ accredited vineyard(s)

Visit
270 Paynters Road,
Blenheim

• Cellar door

Never ending
voyage of discovery

So the name Astrolabe seemed just right when Simon (right) and a group of friends decided to start their own wine label. Simon liked the name's connotations of exploration and adventure and its historical connection with Marlborough.

Like all creative souls he loves to have a free rein, innovating and producing new wines without constraints and with his own label he has that freedom. In 12 Astrolabe vintages, Simon has delivered various interpretations of riesling, a range of sauvignon blancs from different valleys and individual sites in Marlborough, gewürztraminer, pinot gris, pinot noir, two styles of chardonnay and a dessert wine.

Simon's passion has been known to run away with him but he disciplines himself to create three distinct ranges. Voyage is a range of archetypal Marlborough wines, while the Discovery range focuses on the variety offered by grapes grown in Marlborough's different sub-regions. But it is with the Experience range that Simon allows himself license to concentrate on specific parcels of fruit and challenge the usual winemaking processes. For Experience, also read experiment.

Dedicated fans look forward to each new Astrolabe release, eager to share Simon Waghorn's latest wine journey.

Simon Waghorn goes back a long way in the New Zealand wine industry and Marlborough is lucky to have lured him south from Gisborne in the mid 90s. He came originally to join Whitehaven where he is still the winemaker, as he is for a number of other companies who value his spirited approach to his craft. But at Astrolabe, he is on home territory.

An *astrolabe* is the navigational instrument used to plot the position of the stars, after which the French explorer Dumont D'Urville named his bold ship that sailed through the Marlborough Sounds in the early 19th century.

Astrolabe Wines

www.astrolabewines.co.nz

PO Box 1152, Blenheim 7240
T + 64 3 577 6794
info@astrolabewines.co.nz

Owned by Simon Waghorn, Jane Forrest, Sally Lewis & Paul Davenport

Brand
Astrolabe

Varieties Sauvignon Blanc, Pinot Gris, Pinot Noir, Chardonnay, Riesling, Gewürztraminer

Sub-regions
Wairau, Awatere, Kaikoura

Simon loves to have a free rein, innovating and producing new wines without constraints.

Water
into wine

Peter Matthews can remember his father Ellis catching rainbow trout for tea in the Opawa River. Sad to say, the river and its tributaries that used to meander across the Riverby property are long gone, diverted to protect Blenheim from flooding. But the river's importance to the people of this area is remembered in the Riverby logo, a fine rainbow trout.

There is a strong sense of history at Riverby. The homestead, surrounded by magnificent old trees and the remnants of 100 years of farming, was built by Charles Matthews who bought the land in 1898. The homestead is still lived in by members of the Matthews family who manage the vineyard following generations that have grown crops and run sheep on the fertile alluvial soil left behind by the rivers.

Simon Matthews planted the first vines here in 1989 and now 50 hectares are planted in sauvignon blanc, chardonnay, pinot noir, riesling, pinot gris, semillon and syrah. A few paddocks are still retained for sheep that have the job of grazing the vineyards during the winter.

The qualities and characteristics of Riverby fruit owe much to the gravely, free-draining soil and to the use of labour-intensive, low-yield viticultural techniques. The first wine under the Riverby Estate label, a sauvignon blanc, was produced in 1999. Since then, pinot noir, chardonnay, riesling and pinot gris have all been added to the range.

The wines are produced in quite small quantities and mostly exported to Australia and the USA. However, increased production is planned for future years which should mean we see more of the Riverby label in New Zealand.

Riverby Estate

www.riverbyestate.com
Jacksons Road, RD3,
Blenheim 7273
T + 64 21 172 4981
riverby@avenelle.co.nz

Owned by
Riverby Estate Limited

Brand
Riverby Estate

Varieties Sauvignon Blanc, Chardonnay, Pinot Gris, Riesling, Pinot Noir

Sub-region Wairau

SWNZ accredited vineyard(s)

Escaping to the country

You're recently married, you both have good jobs and you have a lifestyle in Wellington that many would give their right arms for. So why would you give it all up to start a vineyard in Marlborough? Love of wine, especially pinot gris, is the simple answer from Dave and Christine Macdonald (right), who had a dream that eventually came true.

In 1989 the Macdonalds bought a small block of land in Marlborough and for three years they commuted, developing their vineyard at weekends and planting pinot gris first of course. "We were living on a breadline budget and a glass of our favourite tipple was a rare treat in those days," recalls Christine. "But we didn't mind and eventually we got brave enough to ditch the city life-belt and make the move to live here permanently"

As a result of all that hard work, the Macdonald's vineyard in Conders Bend Road is the home of Marlborough's oldest pinot gris vines and the source of their boutique, hand crafted wine range which now also includes sauvignon blanc, riesling, gewürztraminer, pinot noir and merlot/malbec.

Dave and Christine have grown a family here too. Blair and Deni provide the name for the wine label, Bladen, and already help out in the business. Their parents still spend much of their time in the vineyard but they also derive great satisfaction from the people side of the business. Amongst the vines they have built a quirky indoor-outdoor tasting room. "Someone comes in knowing very little about wine and leaves with a new understanding and appreciation. I get a buzz out of that," says Dave. "We welcome everyone, and their questions," adds Christine. "We enjoy sharing the little country vineyard experience with our visitors."

So there it is, a dream come true. The Macdonalds look like the cats that got the cream, or rather the city slickers who got their very own supply of pinot gris and a lot more besides.

Bladen Wines

www.bladen.co.nz
PO Box 68,
Renwick 7243
T + 64 3 572 9417
wine@bladen.co.nz

Owned by Dave &
Christine Macdonald

Brand
Bladen

Varieties Sauvignon Blanc,
Pinot Gris, Gewürztraminer,
Riesling, Pinot Noir,
Merlot/Malbec

Sub-region Wairau

Visit
83 Conders Bend Road,
Renwick

• Cellar door

In the footsteps

New owners brought fresh ideas and, in 2005, a striking new tasting room and cellar door building, but the fundamentals remain the same. The drive is always to make the best premium sauvignon blanc, chardonnay, pinot gris and pinot noir.

Chief winemaker Ben Glover (far right) has been at Wither Hills since the first vintage back in 1998. He's a cool, calm, collected guy, and has to be because there is a lot riding on his shoulders. "Well, actually no," says Ben with a cheeky grin. "It's all his problem really." To which General Manager Geoff Matthews (near right) cracks back, "I thought you were the genius!"

These two share the running of Wither Hills which has a long history in the Marlborough wine region and has been owned by Lion Nathan since 2002.

In 1973, local stock and station agent John Marris planted some of the first vines in Marlborough. Later, Brent Marris followed in his father's footsteps founding Wither Hills Vineyards in 1992. Then, in 1999, the two joined forces and launched the Wither Hills wine label as we know it today.

The Marrises are born and bred Marlburians

# of modern pioneers

and Ben Glover is a man of these parts too. After graduating with commerce and oenology degrees, he travelled the world's wine regions, California, France, Italy and Australia, learning his craft before being recruited by Brent Marris for the 1998 vintage. Geoff joined the business in 2002, the year Lion Nathan took over.

New owners brought fresh ideas and, in 2005, a striking new tasting room and cellar door building, but the fundamentals remain the same.

The drive is always to make the best premium sauvignon blanc, chardonnay, pinot gris and pinot noir.

350 hectares of vineyards across the Wairau Valley, with the vines of some now over 20 years old, are presided over by Geoff, who has the last word. "If its going out with Wither Hills on the label it's like it's going out with all our names on it, so we make sure that everything's as perfect as it can be."

Wither Hills
....
www.witherhills.co.nz

211 New Renwick Road,
RD 2, Blenheim 7272
T + 64 3 520 8270
winery@witherhills.co.nz

Owned by
Lion Nathan

Brand Wither Hills

Varieties Sauvignon Blanc,
Chardonnay, Pinot Noir,
Pinot Gris

Sub-regions Wairau,
Southern Valleys

SWNZ accredited vineyard(s)
SWNZ accredited winery

Visit
211 New Renwick Road,
Blenheim

- Cellar door
- Platter lunches
- Picnic area
- Bicycles for hire
- Function venue

No room for the mediocre

"It's about applying art and science in the spirit of give and take... Good stuff in, good stuff out."

At first encounter, Seresin Estate may seem incongruous with the man who owns and inspires it. The logo is a simple handprint, the tasting room understated and stylishly rustic. The marketing material is modest. Michael Seresin, on the other hand, has a reputation for airing his passionate views on the quality of wine, food, art and all things cultural. And he isn't afraid to vocalise his frustrations with aspects of his homeland.

On closer examination however, it is obvious that the Seresin label and the man behind it are totally consistent. An international cinematographer, Michael (right) began Seresin Estate in 1992. Since then, three vineyards have been established, thousands of olive trees and hundreds of native tress have been planted, wetlands have been restored and vegetable gardens now provide fresh food for all the staff.

For a man who couldn't wait to leave New Zealand in his early 20s, the cultivation of the land and the construction of a house in the Marlborough Sounds, have marked a homecoming. During Michael's decades abroad, where he settled in Italy and London, he has been successful in his chosen career and admits that putting down roots again in New Zealand hasn't always been easy. "I get so frustrated with the smallness of New Zealand. But then I go to my house at Waterfall Bay or I come here to the vineyard and despite myself, I do feel at home. I get an enormous amount of satisfaction from working with others to create something quite different to creating a film."

What he has created is 115 hectares of vineyard planted in sauvignon blanc, chardonnay, riesling, pinot gris, gewürztraminer and pinot noir; and a powerful vision which his team strive to real-ise. "Wine and food, amongst other things, to me represent a cultured life. What I aspire to achieve here is to produce the best wine and food that we can." The way to achieve that, as far as Michael is concerned, is by embracing the world of organic

and biodynamic farming and winemaking.

Untouched by chemicals and grown in harmony with natural rhythms, Seresin grapes are hand tended and hand picked, and the wines hand made using gentle and traditional practices. Organic and biodynamic principles are central to the philosophy. The entire estate uses specially formulated biodynamic preparations which, along with natural composts and teas, are used to promote healthy soil and healthy plants.

Estate manager Colin Ross (left) makes it all sound so obvious, "It's about applying art and science in the spirit of give and take. Everything that is wasted in the winemaking process gets recycled back into the soil along with composts made from seaweed, egg shells – anything natural that will enrich the soil and keep the vines in peak condition. Good stuff in, good stuff out."

At harvest time, people come from all over the world to work at Seresin because they want to learn and experience biodynamic vineyard management first hand. Michael likes the idea that what was once considered unorthodox is now proving itself and attracting more and more followers.

"We're not doing it as some smart marketing gimmick," says Michael. "I just believe it is right. If you can make great wine with a light footprint, then why not?"

Seresin Estate

www.seresin.co.nz

PO Box 859,
Blenheim 7240
T + 64 3 572 9408
info@seresin.co.nz

Owned by
Michael Seresin

Brands Seresin, Momo

Varieties Riesling, Chardonnay, Sauvignon Blanc, Gewürztraminer, Pinot Gris, Pinot Noir

Sub-regions
Wairau, Southern Valleys

Full BioGro certified organic vineyard & product

Visit
85 Bedford Road, Renwick

- Cellar door
- Winery and vineyard tours by arrangement
- Vineyard sculpture gallery
- Programme of degustation dinner events

The Kerner Show

Bruce Kerner and his wife Joanne first came to New Zealand in 1992. They were on holiday, having a break from their very urban lives in Los Angeles where both were involved in the television industry. They fell in love with the country, the people, the life, the literature, and of course, the food and the wine. Like so many holidaymakers, they played with idea of never going home.

When they did go home, they went back to work, Bruce as a senior manager of companies making programmes like Judge Judy and Sabrina the Teenage Witch and Joanne as a producer of sitcoms such as Cosby and Grace Under Fire. But the pair could not get New Zealand out of their heads, so in 1995 Bruce was back to figure out how they could make their dream of planting a vineyard and making wine a reality.

Bruce quickly decided that Marlborough was the place to be as the region reminded him of California in the 60s; full of potential and still small enough to be inviting. He bought some land just outside Blenheim. "New Zealand, and Marlborough in particular, offered us a great lifestyle and a chance to make a good product for a growing market, more than could be said of US network television at the time," says Joanne.

Bruce adds drama to the point, "We were at the peak of our respective careers but having seen the handwriting on the tube, I knew that we needed a strong third act on which to end big, not to simply have a lingering denouement before the curtain came down."

For eight years, Bruce and Joanne wound down their media careers, fitting in trips to oversee the start up and development of the estate. They revelled in the culture shock. "We had a one-room cottage on the property and we'd be out in all weathers getting to grips with our new business,"

Kerner Estate Wines

www.kerner.co.nz

57 Fareham Lane
RD1, Blenheim
T + 64 3 572 4446
info@kerner.co.nz

Owned by
Bruce & Joanne Kerner

Brand
Kerner Estate Wines

Varieties
Sauvignon Blanc, Chardonnay, Pinot Noir, Pinot Gris, Pinot Blanc

Sub-region Wairau

says Joanne. "Bruce used to buy me nice jewellery. Now he was buying me things like a frost fighting wind machine and a small tractor!"

Eventually, the dream came true with a permanent move to a new home amongst their vines and olive trees in Marlborough. Today, 22 hectares are planted in sauvignon blanc, pinot noir, pinot gris and chardonnay. And there's pinot blanc too. "One day Bruce told me he was giving me the best gift, two hectares of pinot blanc," recalls Joanne who is very, very fond of pinot blanc. At that time it was not a popular variety in New Zealand and a few years on, it looked like the ultimate sacrifice would have to be made – the pinot blanc would have to be ripped out to make way for something more commercially viable. Then, at the eleventh hour, pinot blanc found a following and started to sell. So much to Joanne's relief, the vines stayed and flourished, just like the Kerners.

Kerner Estate wines, which are made by Brian Bicknell, are made only from estate grown grapes. Quantities are small, around 200 cases a year of each. Success has been rapid with fans in the United Kingdom and New Zealand in particular eagerly anticipating each new release.

The design of the Kerners' new house in the vineyard is American influenced but the lifestyle is distinctly Marlborough. "Twelve years, eight harvests later, we're all sold up in LA and we are here to stay. We still can't believe our luck, to have found this place we love so much and a whole new career to go with it. Thank you New Zealand," says Bruce, his American accent as clear as his delight at having become part of Marlborough's winemaking circle.

"Bruce used to buy me nice jewellery. Now he was buying me things like a frost fighting wind machine and a small tractor!"

Just what the doctor ordered

Way back, when Dr. John Forrest was a biomedical research scientist, he was once told he was too creative. Whilst his risk taking, boundary pushing and innovative thinking might have been a bit much for his employers, it is these characteristics that have proven winning attributes in the wine industry, where John (below) is much more comfortable being his own boss.

Childhood memories of the easy Marlborough lifestyle and an early appreciation of the potential to grow great wine here prompted John and his wife Brigid to look around for somewhere to start their own vineyard. In 1988 they purchased an eight hectare block on the outskirts of Renwick and the move from international scientific careers to new lives in the wine industry was made.

The Forrest's first vintage in 1990 was rewarded with an Air New Zealand wine award and since then they have never looked back. 20 years on, Forrest Estate now spans 80 hectares across seven strategically located vineyards. More than 14 varieties are grown to create a range of over 20 wines.

The company remains wholly owned by

the Forrest family. "We're an unpretentious, quintessentially Kiwi family," says John who uses the word family to encompass the 20 strong staff team that helps make the whole place tick. "Wine making is a team game. I like being the captain and the coach but I need some first rate players and we've always been able to attract the best."

John is still absorbed full-time and hands-on as viticulturist and winemaker, always exploring new wine styles and introducing exotic new varieties to the region, such as chenin blanc and grüner veltliner.

And then there's John's obsession with riesling. Forrest produces six different styles of riesling, from the bone dry to the lusciously sweet. "At heart I'm a wine drinker. I want to produce wines that are enormously pleasurable to drink. Riesling is that and more; it expresses the terroir in which it grows more than any other grape. It can be made successfully in a diversity of styles. It drinks well when youthful and then develops a whole new personality in adulthood."

John's latest riesling is another innovation, this time inspired by his wife's interest in the health benefits of wine. Brigid, a medical doctor by profession, divides her time between the wine business and practice in geriatric medicine. "In recent years we have come to recognise that French people seem to be able to eat a relatively high fat diet without suffering anything like the same rate of heart

In 1988 they purchased an eight hectare block on the outskirts of Renwick and the move from international scientific careers to new lives in the wine industry was made.

disease as other populations. This has been attributed to the glass of wine that tends to be a normal part of French meals. So, I wondered whether we could produce a white wine with lower than usual alcohol content that could be enjoyed little and often; a wine that was just as appealing as the very best in our range."

Of course, Doctor John rose to the challenge and the result is The Doctors' Riesling. Made in the German Kabinett style it has only 8.5% alcohol compared to 12-14% for standard wines. It meets with Doctor Brigid's approval. "This is a very poised and balanced riesling with flavours of lemon blossoms and golden apples, wonderful with light meals, fish, and ideal for lunch. At just over one unit of alcohol per glass this is my prescription for the good of your mind, body and soul."

So has John achieved his quest to craft the perfect riesling? No, he is not about to rest on his laurels just yet. "You never stop learning. If you have the courage to apply what you learn you will move forward. There's always more to strive for."

Forrest Estate Winery

www.forrest.co.nz

19 Blicks Road,
Renwick 7204
T + 64 3 572 9084
info@forrestwines.co.nz

Owned by
Drs John & Brigid Forrest

Brands Forrest, Forrest The Valleys, The Doctors', John Forrest Collection, Stonewall, Belmonte, Heart of Stone
Varieties Sauvignon Blanc, Chenin Blanc, Chardonnay, Viognier, Riesling, Arneis, Gewürztraminer, Pinot Gris, Merlot, Pinot Noir
Sub-regions Wairau, Awatere, Southern Valleys
SWNZ accredited vineyard(s)

Visit
Off SH6, 1km
north of Renwick.

• Cellar door
• Picnic area

A life measured in vintages

It's a warm summer's day and the visitors are glad of the shade offered by the trees in the garden at Hunter's winery. Gardening is second only to wine on Jane Hunter's priority list and the latest plantings of endangered native shrubs and plants are doing well. Restaurant diners are relaxing with their pick of the Hunter's wine list over lunch and Jane (far right) is in the vineyard, deep in conversation with winemaker Gary Duke (near right) and viticulturist Bryan Vickery. They are making final decisions on arrangements for the harvest which looks likely to begin within days.

Jane's vintage experience began as a child growing up on a vineyard just north of the Barossa Valley in South Australia.

"It doesn't matter how many vintages you have been through," says Jane, "it's always nail biting until you know the grapes are all in and in good condition." Jane's vintage experience began as a child growing up on a vineyard just north of the Barossa Valley in South Australia. After studying viticulture at university, Jane decided to gain practical experience overseas and came to Marlborough when the region's wine industry was in its infancy. She has been here ever since.

Though there are many women involved in the wine industry and many who run wine companies with their partners, there are few in New Zealand who lead a wine company solo as Jane does. It was not meant to be this way though. In 1983, Jane was in charge of viticulture at Montana when her husband Ernie started up a small winery, one of the first in Marlborough. Hunter's sauvignon blanc quickly made a big impression on the world market but just as things were taking off, Ernie was killed in an accident and Jane was left holding the fledgling company together. What an amazing job she did. 20 odd years on and Hunter's is everything Ernie could possibly have dreamed of.

Sauvignon blanc is still to the fore, but the Hunter's range also includes gewürztraminer, chardonnay, riesling and pinot noir. All meet Ernie and Jane's standards of quality, consistency and value. The wines have won many awards over the years and Jane has also won many, for her contribution to New Zealand's wine industry. She was awarded an OBE in 1993, an honorary doctorate of science from Massey University in 1997 and in 2003 received the inaugural Women in Wine Award at the International Wine & Spirit Competition in London.

Gary Duke has been at Hunter's since 1991. He and the other members of Jane's team make sure all is looked after at home while Jane travels the world promoting Marlborough wine and breaking into new markets such as Vietnam, Malaysia and Dubai. Another country may soon be added to the list as Jane is one of a group of New Zealand wine leaders that has recently been on a mission to India. There's always something new to do.

Marking the entrance to the Hunter's winery complex is a quarter acre or so of vines which look quite different to anything you are likely to see elsewhere in Marlborough. They are thick stemmed, gnarled and trained over a high horizontal trellis. "These are a bit of our history," says Jane. "Ernie planted these right beside the road, so that locals could see what vines looked like, because in those days there weren't that many around." That was 30 years ago. Marlborough has come a long way since then and Hunter's with it.

Hunter's Wines

. . . .

www.hunters.co.nz

PO Box 128, Renwick 7243
T + 64 3 572 8489
wine@hunters.co.nz

Owned by
Jane Hunter

Brand
Hunter's

Varieties Breidecker,
Gewürztraminer, Riesling,
Chardonnay, Sauvignon Blanc,
Pinot Gris, Pinot Noir, Merlot.

Sub-region
Wairau

SWNZ accredited vineyard(s)

Visit
Rapaura Road,
Blenheim

• Cellar door
• Hunter's Garden Café
• Artist in residence
• Sculpture display
• Native garden

47

Small is beautiful

ean-Charles and Marguerite Van Hove are originally from Belgium. Their accents reflect their backgrounds and their vine growing and winemaking techniques are clearly European. But there's a very strong Kiwi spirit flowing in the veins of these two modern wine pioneers.

Building on a vision from many years ago, Jean-Charles and Marguerite are now living their dream of hand crafting small quantities of sauvignon blanc and pinot noir on the south bank of the Awatere River.

Their vineyard sits on a gravel terrace and takes advantage of a terroir undiscovered until recently. Free-draining soils combined with a dry and sunny climate results in low vine vigour and the ability to reach full aromatic maturity. High-density planting, Guyot pruning and low, controlled yield are practices brought with them from the old country, together with a taste for subtle yet rich, textural, complex flavours.

But it is their can-do approach and keen sense of humour that has brought them to where they are today. They do just about everything themselves and as the children, Sibylle and Marin, grew up they were involved too. The Van Hoves' particular blend of old world and new world approaches is labour intensive and meticulous. Most of the vineyard work, including picking, is done by hand as they believe this brings enormous benefits in the quality of the wine.

Marguerite, whose grandfather was a wine wholesaler in Brussels, has an intimate knowledge of the vineyard and a passionate appreciation for wine. She spends most of her time either in the vineyard or on the road, anywhere from Amsterdam to New York, from Copenhagen to Wellington, introducing the wines to top restaurants.

Jean-Charles, who has a soil science and viticulture background and gained his wine

making experience at various Bordeaux chateaux, opens the door of a large shed to reveal what has to be one of the smallest on-site wineries in the region. "Of course, if we were sensible we'd be making the wine in a shared facility, but this way we have full control over the process, meaning we don't make any compromise on quality. The winery is probably better equipped than our house!" he says, laughing.

The company's logo, an art deco dancing figure, signifies the poise, elegance, strength, balance and purity of the wine, as well as old world experience combined with new world innovation.

With seven vintages behind them, to which there has been an excellent response, Jean-Charles

Their can-do approach and keen sense of humour has brought them to where they are today.

and Marguerite are exhilarated with what they have achieved and excited about the future. But small definitely means beautiful. They want to remain small scale and quality focused, proud to maintain their annual production at about 5,000 cases. "We want to stay self-sufficient, family run, doing things ourselves, in our own way, to make the best wine we possibly can," says Jean-Charles. "That is our modest contribution to everything fabulous that Marlborough has to offer which we enjoy so much."

Clos Marguerite

www.closmarguerite.co.nz

PO Box 7, Seddon 7247
T + 64 3 575 7721
info@closmarguerite.co.nz

Owned by Jean-Charles & Marguerite Van Hove

Brand
Clos Marguerite

Varieties
Sauvignon Blanc, Pinot Noir

Sub-region
Awatere

Nothing left to chance

Ask for directions to Cloudy Bay winery and a local might suggest you just look out for people playing Russian roulette with the traffic as they try to get a picture of themselves under the iconic Cloudy Bay sign, or more bizarre still, get out of their cars to kiss the ground.

Cloudy Bay is one of the oldest names in the Marlborough wine business which might account for some of its celebrity status, but it was also one of the earliest Marlborough wine companies to achieve a strong presence in the United Kingdom market. UK wine drinkers often associate their first experience of new world wine with a bottle of Cloudy Bay.

Kevin Judd, pictured above centre with senior winemaker Eveline Fraser and winemaker Nick Lane, is chief winemaker and a director of the company. He has been at Cloudy Bay since its first vintage in 1985. He even took the photograph of the Richmond Ranges for the original label. Asked what the secret to success has been, he immediately says, "Quality. I know that word seems to have lost its meaning, but it still means a lot to us. We take serious care and attention at every step of the process, in the vineyard and in the winery, and right through to marketing and meeting our visitors."

Looking around, you can see that attention to detail is something that runs through the whole operation. Everything is sparkling clean, tidy, cared for. Kevin's disciplined photographer's eye seems to have been at work in every aspect of the winery complex, which welcomes thousands of international visitors every year. A table set for a formal tasting in the barrel hall has every glass immaculately polished and perfectly positioned. The gardens are neatly manicured with places to sit and swap 'my first glass of Cloudy Bay' stories and sample the new and limited release wines that are not available back home.

Attention to detail is something that runs through the whole operation.

"There's no doubt about it, we made our name with sauvignon blanc and it is still our flagship wine, but we are equally proud of the rest of our portfolio, which includes chardonnay, pinot noir, a small selection of aromatic wines and our sparking wine, Pelorus," says Kevin.

Nearly 25 years ago, Cloudy Bay was a place to go fishing and Kevin Judd was newly arrived from Australia, never dreaming of where his move would take him. Today the future looks as good as it has ever done as the company exports to over 30 countries and continues to expand its range.

Cloudy Bay
. . . .
www.cloudybay.co.nz

PO Box 376, Blenheim 7240
T + 64 3 520 9140
info@cloudybay.co.nz

Owned by
Moët Hennessy

Brands
Cloudy Bay, Pelorus
Varieties
Sauvignon Blanc,
Chardonnay, Pinot Noir,
Riesling, Gewürztraminer,
Sub-region Wairau

SWNZ accredited vineyard(s)
SWNZ accredited winery

Visit
Jacksons Road,
Blenheim

• Cellar door

On hallowed ground

The name Saint Clair is an old version of the name Sinclair, after James Sinclair who built one of the first homes in Blenheim and was closely associated with the development of the town.

Sinclair's family were early settlers of the land that Neal and Judy Ibbotson bought in 1973, when Montana and other farmers had not long started to plant grapes. "So instead of running sheep, cattle and pigs on the farm as we had intended, we decided we'd give grapes a go."

It seems entirely fitting that the name of Neal and Judy's wine label should be that of a female saint when you hear the story of their early days, planting out the home vineyard.

To keep the family finances afloat, Neal kept his job as a farm consultant, so it fell to Judy to do much of the physical work, fitting the work around the needs of her young children. In the school holidays, the children helped too.

The Ibbotsons quickly became respected contract growers but they didn't make the move to producing their own wine until the children reached their teens. "We held our breath and took the plunge. We wondered whether we'd made the right decision, but not for long," says Judy. Their first winemaker was Kim Crawford later followed by Matt Thomson who had been at Saint Clair right from the first vintage in 1994. Since then

The company has developed its own quality-measurement system to grade wines during the winemaking process

Matt has become a leading winemaker working vintages all over the world. These days he divides his year between Marlborough and Italy.

At harvest time Matt and senior winemaker Hamish Clark (left) spend much of their time out in the vineyards monitoring the differences in flavour between grape bunches and between different sites in Rapaura and the Wairau, Waihopai, Awatere and Omaka valleys, plus a new site for sauvignon blanc in Benmorven. Everything is done to ensure that grapes are picked at the optimum time and the right fruit from the best locations is chosen for each individual variety.

Saint Clair produces sauvignon blanc, pinot gris, chardonnay, riesling, gewürztraminer, viognier, pinot noir, syrah and merlot, and the company has developed its own quality-measurement system to grade wines during the winemaking process, to identify the Reserve and Pioneer Block wines.

The Ibbotsons and Saint Clair have come a long way since Judy and her friends planted that first block. 4,000 cases in 1994 has now grown to over 200,000 cases every year, exported to over 50 countries, including most recently, India and Russia.

Saint Clair is still very much a family business. Children Tony, Sarina and Julie have flown the nest and are pursuing careers away from home, but they are still part of the team. Tony is responsible for all creative design and Sarina and Julie work on sales and marketing.

"We have fond memories of the early days," says Neal, "but we're always excited about the future, building on the success of Marlborough's sauvignon blanc and the other varieties we have added. We've never regretted choosing grapes over pigs!"

Saint Clair Family Estate

www.saintclair.co.nz

PO Box 970, Blenheim 7240
T + 64 3 578 8695
wine@saintclair.co.nz

Owned by
Neal & Judy Ibbotson

Brand
Saint Clair

Varieties Sauvignon Blanc,
Chardonnay, Riesling, Viognier,
Pinot Gris, Gewürztraminer,
Merlot, Pinot Noir, Syrah

Sub-regions
Wairau, Awatere,
Southern Valleys

Visit
Corner Rapaura
& Selmes Road,
Blenheim

• Cellar door
• Café
• Cottage
  accommodation
• Winery tours by
  arrangement

The history of Drylands is liberally peppered with famous winemaking names. Ewan Robinson was the far-sighted grape grower who planted some of the first vines in Marlborough in the early 1980s. Ewan named his Wairau Valley vineyard Drylands, a simple description of the dry, stony soils that were to prove so perfect for sauvignon blanc. Next came the Selaks family followed by the Nobilo family, then Hardys. Today the company is owned by international drinks company Constellation Brands, but it is still run as a stand-alone entity and managed by Darryl Woolley, winemaker since 1985.

An Australian, Darryl, pictured standing with Ollie Davidson, Viticulture Manager and Matthew Sheridan, Vineyards Manager, started his career at wineries in the Clare Valley. In the late 70s he came to New Zealand to work for Corbans in Gisborne. Moving to Drylands in 1985 he earned his stripes as a pioneer of classic Marlborough

Thinking globally, acting locally

sauvignon blanc and he has since been responsible for Drylands' success across all its varieties.

For someone like Darryl, still obsessed by making wine after more years in the business than he cares to recall, there are plenty of advantages to working with such a large organisation. "First of all we have the investment to provide up to the minute equipment, the latest technology and increased capacity and my team and I get to concentrate on what we do best. We can be absolutely focused on making Drylands wines at Drylands, knowing that somewhere out there, there is an international

marketing team getting the wines noticed in all the right places," says Darryl.

And then he remembers that his face is part of the marketing campaign. He laughs. "If the marketing gurus say my photograph on a billboard or in a magazine is what they want, then I'm fine with that. Just so long as I can spend most of my time here, in Marlborough, looking after the wine. And yes, I am getting used to those puzzled looks that say 'Where have I seen that guy before?'"

Drylands Marlborough
. . . .

www.drylands.co.nz

PO Box 260, Blenheim 7240
T + 64 3 570 5252
cellardoor@drylands.co.nz

Owned by Constellation New Zealand

Brand
Drylands

Varieties Sauvignon Blanc, Riesling, Chardonnay, Pinot Gris, Pinot Noir, Merlot

Sub-regions Wairau, Awatere, Southern Valleys

SWNZ accredited vineyard(s)
SWNZ accredited winery

Visit
Hammerichs Road, Rapaura, Blenheim

• Cellar door
• Drylands Restaurant

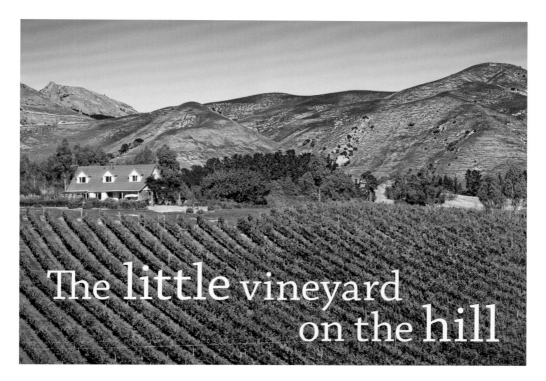

The little vineyard on the hill

The Sentinel vineyard stands out among the bare folds of the upper Brancott Valley. This is grape growing on a truly boutique scale. At just nine hectares the Sentinel vineyard must be one of the smallest in Marlborough producing grapes for its owners' own commercial label. Neil and Lyn Berry, whose family have lived in Marlborough since 1860, planted out their tiny vineyard with sauvignon blanc reparier gloire rootstock to emphasise flavour over quantity. The clay hillside is well positioned for the Marlborough sunshine. The intense mineral content of these soils and carefully restricted irrigation produce a harvest from which Sentinel's single vineyard sauvignon blanc is made. The winemaker's philosophy is one of minimal handling to allow the vineyard's particular characteristics to be fully expressed.

Neil and Lyn are very proud of what they have achieved. "We think our little vineyard is very special. The soils of Marlborough are so varied; every vineyard has its own characteristics which come through in the wines. Our grapes are different to the grapes from the vineyard just down the road," says Neil. "Staying this size means Lyn and I can supervise everything ourselves and truly feel that the end product is the quality we are looking for."

Sentinel Vineyard

www.sentinelvineyard.co.nz

221 Wrekin Road,
RD2, Blenheim 7272
T + 64 3 572 9143
enquiries@sentinelvineyard.com

Owned by Neil & Lyn Berry

Brand
Sentinel

Variety Sauvignon Blanc

Sub-region
Southern Valleys

SWNZ accredited vineyard(s)

Visit
221 Wrekin Road,
Fairhall

• Tastings by appointment

The heart of the old world, the pulse of the new

This is the story of a journey from the heart of the old world into the pulse of the new; the story of Hans and Therese Herzog who established a famous and successful winery in Switzerland, then moved it all to Marlborough, driven by pure passion and the desire to create great wine.

Hans Herzog's family winemaking history stretches back over four centuries. Records show that in 1630, Hans' ancestor, Heinrich Herzog, pressed a ring bearing the Herzog crest into the sealing wax on an agreement to purchase a hillside vineyard high in Switzerland's Rhine Valley.

Following in the footsteps of generations before him, Hans was destined for a life of wine and in 1967 he entered the Swiss Wine University of Wadenswil. The lengthy and rigorous training in viticulture and oenology involved academic study and practical experience in wineries, vineyards and farms. 14 years later he emerged, dreaming of making truly amazing red wines.

Hypnotized by the great Burgundies and inspired by his experience with Bordeaux varieties, Hans knew that he needed to break with the Swiss tradition of müller thurgau and pinot noir planted precariously on steep vineyards if he was to achieve his dream. So began a long search for flatter, rolling land; terroir where the modern French varieties would thrive.

In the 13 years it took to find that perfect piece of land, Hans' winery and vineyard, Taggenberg near Zurich, became a huge success and Therese, having left her computing career behind, established a winery restaurant that quickly gained a Michelin star and a Europe-wide reputation.

Then, on a second visit to New Zealand, the lure of an apple orchard on the boundary of the Wairau river in Marlborough proved too great to resist. In 1994 the Herzogs bought the 12 hectare block on Jeffries Road. The conditions were everything Hans had been searching for; hot days, cool nights and flat, dark brown earth peppered with granite beside the sand and stones of the riverbed.

Pinot noir, cabernet sauvignon, cabernet franc, merlot, malbec, montepulciano, chardonnay, pinot gris and viognier were planted. Then on Christmas Day 1999, Hans, Therese, their Taggenberg chef and maitre d' bid goodbye to their businesses, families and friends in Switzerland and took off for a new life in Marlborough.

Why leave a successful business and enviable reputation to start all over again in New Zealand? "Terroir," whispers Hans, eyes twinkling with the satisfaction of one who has found exactly what he was looking for. *Terroir* – that magical combination of soil, exposure and microclimate that gives a vineyard site its unique complexion. Here the grapes find their true expression in the wines, and such purity of flavour requires simply the very best fruit. Hans lives and breathes the vineyard, taking full advantage of its natural warmth and protection from frost; constantly tending, leaf-plucking, bunch-thinning, paring

On Christmas Day 1999, Hans, Therese, their Taggenberg chef and maitre d' bid goodbye to their businesses, families and friends in Switzerland and took off for a new life in Marlborough.

down the crop until there is very little left. What is left has the goodness, warmth, light and indeed magic, all to itself.

No pesticides or chemical fertilizers are used and in the winery Hans takes the same approach. His non-interventional philosophy allows wines to undergo long, cool fermentation with wild yeasts; here old-world methods, passion and experience go hand in hand with scientific analysis and technology. Temperature-controlled, tiny stainless steel tanks ensure wines are kept at the optimum temperature. French oak barriques

are stacked in the cool, dark barrel cellar, and the wines are left unfined and unfiltered to preserve intact the complexity and structure they have become famous for.

Alongside the winery, Therese has once again created a restaurant of international repute where her expertise and the skills of her "cherished chefs" combine to provide a dining experience where Herzog wines can be enjoyed as the winemaker intended – with great food.

The Herzog story continues with each passing harvest. Hans leads the way with new grape varieties such as nebbiolo, tempranillo, arneis, rousanne and zweigelt. Bottles lie waiting to come of age, mellow enough to leave home to delight those passing through and friends and fans on the other side of the world. Hans and Therese work their magic from year to year, as they quietly dig their own roots deeper into Marlborough's soil.

Hans Herzog Estate
....
www.herzog.co.nz

81 Jeffries Road,
RD3, Blenheim 7272
T + 64 3 572 8770
info@herzog.co.nz

Owned by
Hans & Therese Herzog

Brands
Herzog, Hans Herzog, Hans
Varieties
Sauvignon Blanc, Riesling, Pinot Gris, Chardonnay, Gewürztraminer, Viognier, Pinot Noir, Tempranillo, Merlot, Nebbiolo, Montepulciano, Barbera, Zweigelt, Cabernet Franc

Sub-region Wairau

SWNZ accredited vineyard(s)

Visit 81 Jeffries Road, Blenheim
• Cellar door
• Winery tours
• Herzog Restaurant
• Bistro
• Gardens
• Cooking classes
• Kitchen confidentials
• Wine dinners
• Vineyard cottage accommodation

Champagne-maker Daniel Le Brun is busy on the packing line, working alongside the team putting bottles of bubbly into cases for export. He has a list of other things to do before the day is out. Daniel cannot resist being involved in every step of the winemaking process. He never stops even though he has been around the Marlborough wine business since 1980 and could surely be forgiven for taking it a bit easier these days.

"That's just not how we are," says Daniel's wife, Adele. "We are still very hands-on. At present our son Remy is working with us so we have to keep up with all his youthful energy." Daughter Virginie

It's all about bubbles

completes the No. 1 family. Virginie is a television presenter in Auckland but also assists Adele with marketing the wines, and is always keen to do her stint when she is home in Marlborough.

"Of course, we could have moved away from méthode traditionelle," says Daniel when he is at last persuaded to take a break. "But I came to Marlborough carrying twelve generations of Champagne-making tradition from France. It's in my blood and why not specialise in what you are really good at?"

Méthode traditionelle is the generic name for the wine style that originated in the Champagne region of France. The grapes are hand picked, pressed in whole bunches and then fermented in steel tanks until spring when the wine is bottled and gets a shot of yeast and sugar to start the fermentation again. Then the magic begins. The wine is matured for two years during which time it is ever so gently, ever so slightly turned and tilted every day. It is during this second fermentation that the bubbles appear. When the winemaker declares it is time, the sediment, which is resting in the neck of the bottles, is disgorged. Then the bottles are re-corked and dressed up in their wire closures and labels.

Finally, the bottles are lovingly placed in their cases and the team at No. 1 Family Estate say "au revoir" to more bubbles leaving on their way to celebrations all over the world.

No.1 Family Estate

www.no1familyestate.co.nz
169 Rapaura Road,
Renwick 7273
T + 64 3 572 9876
marketing@no1familyestate.co.nz

Owned by
Adele & Daniel Le Brun

Brand
No. 1 Family Estate

Varieties
Chardonnay, Pinot Noir,
Meunier

Sub-region
Wairau

Visit
169 Rapaura Road, Renwick

• Cellar door

A good keen man

Ross Lawson (right) is a man of action. He grew up on farms, first in Kaikoura, then in Marlborough. As a young man he headed off to make his own way, mustering, shearing, working for the shearers' union, hunting possums and building swimming pools. By the time he and his wife Barbara planted their first vines in 1980, putting them amongst the pioneer growers of Marlborough, Ross had acquired a formidable stock of skills and experience. For 12 years Ross and Barbara learned everything there was to learn about growing grapes, which they sold to the wine companies. But by 1992 the novelty was wearing off and they were looking for more of a challenge, so they founded their own label, Lawson's Dry Hills.

True to form, they managed their first vintage, made from 15 tonnes of gewürztraminer grapes, in an old tin shed at the back of their house. The Lawson's range now also includes sauvignon blanc, chardonnay, riesling, pinot gris and pinot noir, and although the shed is still proudly standing, these days the wines are made in rather smarter premises across the yard. The Lawson's label has been a success story from the start, beyond what the couple could possibly have imagined. Tonnage has risen to 700 tonnes and the wines are exported to over 20 countries.

"Making and selling wines that we are proud of is a great thing," says Ross, "but there's always something more to do." By the end of the 90s a new challenge was exercising Ross's restless mind; how to overcome the problem of wines being 'corked'. In 2001, he and a handful of fellow wine industry leaders formed the Screwcap Wine Seal Initiative and Ross believes that Lawson's was the first company in the world to bottle 100% of its production under metal screwcap.

"And don't let anyone tell you we've lost the fun of opening the bottle since we got rid of corks!" says chief winemaker, Marcus Wright. Marcus deftly demonstrates the right way to release the screwcap – grip the cap in one hand, fingers together, and the base of the bottle in the other, fingers spread, then twist both hands in opposite directions, confidently, and with flair. It works.

Lawson's Dry Hills
....
www.lawsonsdryhills.co.nz

PO Box 4020, Blenheim 7242
T + 64 3 578 7674
wine@lawsonsdryhills.co.nz

Owned by
Ross & Barbara Lawson

Brand Lawson's Dry Hills

Varieties Sauvignon Blanc, Riesling, Pinot Gris, Pinot Noir Chardonnay, Gewürztraminer,

Sub-regions
Wairau, Southern Valleys

SWNZ accredited vineyard(s)
SWNZ accredited winery,

Visit
Alabama Road, Blenheim

• Cellar door
• Winery tours

At the sign of the rooster

The Vavasour name is weighted with some serious history. The family can trace its ancestry back to 11th century Normandy in France and 'tis said that one of their number was a taster for William the Conqueror.

Vavasours settled in the Awatere Valley in the 1890s, and a century later Peter Vavasour and a group of farming friends developed the first vineyard in the valley.

Vavasour's viticulturist, Allan Croker, relishes the challenge of growing in difficult conditions, "It's dry and windy. In easier conditions, grape vines produce large yields, but ours produce small, concentrated crops." These grapes are the stuff of award winning wines. Foresight, perseverance and patience pays off.

Chief winemaker Glenn Thomas, originally from Australia, has been with the company since the first vintage, and his second in command, Stu Marfell, goes back a long way too. He was there at the first vintage with his mother, who was helping with the harvest.

The name Vavasour and the rooster logo are recognised world-wide as synonymous with superb Marlborough wines.

Over the last 20 years, the wine venture has added new chapters to nearly two centuries of Vavasour farming history, and as the company continues to develop, more will no doubt be added in the future.

Vavasour Wines
....
www.vavasour.com

PO Box 72, Seddon 7247
T + 64 3 575 7481
info@vavasour.com

Owned by
Privately held

Brands
Vavasour, Dashwood,
Redwood Pass

Varieties Sauvignon Blanc,
Pinot Gris, Pinot Noir,
Chardonnay, Riesling

Sub-regions Wairau, Awatere

SWNZ accredited vineyard(s)
SWNZ accredited winery

Visit
1549 Redwood Pass
Road, Lower Dashwood,
Awatere Valley

• Cellar door

Worth waiting for

Regular visitors to Fromm's tasting room might be able to guess which wine is being made from the music drifting through from the winery. "It's definitely Verdi when we're working with the Fromm Vineyard pinot noir, while the Clayvin Vineyard chardonnay is more like a Bellini belcanto," says winemaker Hätsch Kalberer. "And we're into jazz too, the freer the better when it comes to making the La Strada range."

Hätsch and fellow winemaker William Hoare (right) share a love of music that has stood the test of time, which reflects their thinking about wine. Most Fromm wines are aged for two or three years before they are released for sale and they are made to be enjoyed for years into the future.

Hätsch, who has been making wine in New Zealand for almost three decades, still carries and cares about the values of his native Switzerland where wine, like food, is a very important part of everyday culture, cellaring is common and people collect wine, patiently waiting until it has developed maturity, depth, and personality. "We are making wines that will evolve over perhaps 10 or 15 years and bring a smile to the face of the buyer who has had the foresight to keep it all that time," says Hätsch. "Which is why we use corks. We don't want the bottle to be completely sealed because age-worthy wines benefit from breathing a little, so natural corks are the most suitable closures for Fromm wines. They feel good too."

The results of applying winemaking traditions from Europe in the young growing region of Marlborough have captured the attention of wine collectors the world over, many of whom become well known to the team at Fromm where the personal touch is all part of the service. And if you are lucky enough to meet one of the winemakers, they might just give you a recommendation for a musical accompaniment to the wine of your choice.

Fromm Winery
....
www.frommwinery.co.nz

Godfrey Road,
RD2, Blenheim 7272
T + 64 3 572 9355
lastrada@frommwinery.co.nz

Owned by
Fromm & Partner Limited

Brands
Fromm, La Strada,
William Thomas

Varieties
Pinot Noir, Chardonnay,
Riesling, Malbec, Pinot Gris,
Sauvignon Blanc, Syrah

Sub-regions
Wairau, Southern Valleys

Visit
Godfrey Road, Blenheim

• Cellar door

Like a kid in a candy store

Brian Bicknell is literally jumping around with frustration and talking to a sofa. "I must have measured it wrong," he says as he and his assistant try to fit the thing into its designated space in the newly designed tasting room. This man's a perfectionist but he's ready to admit his own mistakes. "You don't get anywhere if you don't take risks, and if you take risks you fall over sometimes." He's laughing now and still jumping around. The excitement is rising everywhere with the promise of a big harvest and high quality fruit. Brian Bicknell (right) is absolutely fizzing with energy as he shows you around the winery which is being prepared for vintage. This is only the second year he has had a winery of his own and he just can't wait for the grapes to arrive.

Brian has made wine all over the world but Marlborough is definitely home, even though he still can't resist doing the odd vintage in Chile where he has long standing wine connections. He has been based mainly in Marlborough since 1996. At that time many Marlborough wines were blended from grapes that came from different valleys, but Brian was more interested in making wines from particular growing environments and single vineyards.

He continued to work for various wine companies while playing with the idea of starting his own. Then, in 2001, the decision was finally made. "My father was diagnosed with a terminal illness and being faced with my own mortality was the impetus that I needed to finally start Mahi." For a few years it was a case of fitting Mahi in around ongoing commitments. The operation was run on a shoestring and wine quantities were so small that stocks sold easily by word of mouth.

The excitement is rising everywhere, with the promise of a big harvest and high quality fruit.

Brian began approaching growers with vineyards that had the particular characteristics he was looking for. "I always want to make wines that speak of their origins," says Brian. The first grapes came from a 1.5 hectare parcel of sauvignon blanc and pinot noir in the Byrne vineyard in the Conders Bend area. In 2003 another vineyard, Twin Valleys, was selected, as it was in another distinctive part of the Wairau Valley with slightly cooler temperatures and longer ripening times. And in 2004, an

opportunity to take some sauvignon blanc from the Francis vineyard closer to the sea presented itself. The portfolio of vineyards was growing, and along with it Brian's impatience to be out there with his own winery.

2006 was the year to go for it, as the salary was abandoned and the winery was bought. "It was really scary for us," Brian admits, looking anything but scared as he proudly proceeds with the tour including the cellars which will soon be the scene of the harvest party.

Any day now he and his team will be hand sorting grapes, loading the presses with the white varieties and hand plunging the pinot noir which is likely to be bottled unfiltered, allowing the wine to really show what it is made of. Fermentation is most often done with the indigenous yeasts that arrive on the grapes, and if barrels are used, they will be French as these give a more savoury character to the wines.

Looking forward, Brian will continue to seek out vineyards that fit his style but Mahi will remain at a size that allows him and his close team to stay intimately connected with the vineyards and wines. *Mahi* means 'our work' or 'our craft' in Māori and you can see why it was chosen for this label. "Everyone here is a wine fanatic, we're obsessed. It's more like a vocation than a job," says Brian, before bounding off to tackle the next thing on the list.

Mahi
....
www.mahiwine.co.nz

PO Box 33, Renwick 7204
T + 64 3 572 8859
info@mahiwine.co.nz

Owned by
Brian & Nicola Bicknell

Brand
Mahi

Varieties Sauvignon Blanc, Gewürztraminer, Chardonnay, Pinot Gris, Pinot Noir

Sub-regions Wairau, Southern Valleys, Awatere

SWNZ accredited vineyard(s)

Visit
9 Terrace Road, Renwick

● Cellar door
● Winery tours

A picnic of goat's milk cheese, duck paté, crusty bread and a glass of sauvignon blanc, sitting in the sunshine near a pretty wooden church. No, we're not in France but in a Marlborough vineyard that has more than a touch of France about it.

Clos Henri vineyard is owned and run by the Bourgeois family whose history and reputation as growers of sauvignon blanc and pinot noir, in the Sancerre and Pouilly-Fumé regions of France, goes back 10 generations.

Passionate about these two varieties, the family set out to discover other places in the world where they might apply their know-how and experience. In 2000 they settled on Marlborough, New Zealand. A specific 100 hectare hillside site in the Wairau Valley was chosen for its three different soil types, perfectly suited to sauvignon blanc and pinot noir.

In 2001 the first vines were planted in the Bourgeois' signature high density, 5000 vines per hectare method. So was born Clos Henri – *clos* being the French traditional word for a single vineyard that is perceived as a terroir jewel, and *Henri* being the name of the family patriarch.

In 2003 the family came across an unused church in the nearby village of Ward. This provided a very special link between Marlborough and the Bourgeois' home village of Chavignol, which has a church with which Bourgeois wines

are associated. The church was restored and has become the centrepiece of the estate and the image for its distinctive logo.

Today, the Bourgeois family has achieved its ambition to arrange a marriage between French and New Zealand winemaking. The honeymoon may be over, but the couple look set to celebrate their union year after year with each new release of Clos Henri sauvignon blanc and pinot noir.

Vive la Nouvelle Zélande!

Clos Henri Vineyard

www.closhenri.com
PO Box 535,
Blenheim 7240
T + 64 3 572 7923
contact@closhenri.com

Owned by
Domaine Henri Bourgeois

Brands
Clos Henri, Bel Echo

Varieties
Sauvignon Blanc,
Pinot Noir

Sub-region
Wairau

Visit
639 State Highway 63,
West Coast Road
• Cellar door
• Café
• Delicatessen from France
• Domaine Henri Bougeois
  French wines for sale

Hidden treasure

Johanneshof Cellars, between Picton and Blenheim, is Marlborough's northernmost winery. Perched in a fold in the hills, with pinot noir vines running over the ridge behind, the butter-coloured buildings look as though they have been plucked straight out of central Europe, as well they might, for that is where the Johanneshof story starts.

Edel Everling, a fifth generation winemaker from the Rhine wine region of Germany, and fellow winemaker Warwick Foley, a fifth generation New Zealander, first met at Te Kauwhata Wine Research Station near Auckland. Later they both studied viticulture and oenology at Geisenheim University and after working in a number of German wineries, the pair headed to Marlborough with a grand plan to do their own thing.

In 1991 they set up Johanneshof Cellars as a boutique operation, sourcing fruit from their small home vineyard, which is set out on European lines and not irrigated, and carefully selected Marlborough contract growers. Johanneshof was possibly the first winery in the region to concentrate on gewürztraminer and pinot gris, with a fruity Germanic riesling getting early attention too. Their range also includes sauvignon blanc, pinot noir, chardonnay and méthode traditionnelle as well as grape brandy and grappa.

The most remarkable feature of the Johanneshof property is an underground rock cellar, the first of its kind in New Zealand. Warwick turns the key, opens the huge doors and the cool air hits you. Tunnelled into the solid sandstone hillside, the cellar is 50 metres long and 20 metres deep and provides ideal conditions for the maturation of wines in French barriques and German barrels and on Champagne riddling racks.

Outside again, the afternoon sun counters the cellar's chill and Edel's sunflowers, a reminder of her childhood home, nod happily in the breeze.

Johanneshof Cellars

www.johanneshof.co.nz

RD3, Koromiko, Blenheim 7273
T + 64 3 573 7035
wines@johanneshof.co.nz

Owned by Warwick Foley
& Edel Everling

Brand
Johanneshof Cellars

Varieties
Gewürztraminer, Riesling,
Sauvignon Blanc, Pinot Gris,
Pinot Noir

Sub-region
Wairau

Visit
State Highway 1,
Koromiko,
9kms south of Picton

• Cellar door
• Underground cellar

Royal family connections

It's baking hot and still. A moving dust cloud marks the progress of Mike Just's classic car along the Omaka Valley. How on earth do they grow grapes way up here? "Very well, and without any irrigation," is Mike's reply when he arrives home. Mike looks like the archetypal hard man with a soft centre. He's a man who gets enthusiastic about a lot of things; his family, his cars, his vineyard, his wines and ... England in the middle ages.

In the corner of Mike and Paula Just's living room stands a full suit of armour, now rarely worn but once a regular weekend outfit when Mike was taking part in medieval re-enactments. He has traced his ancestry back to King Edward III who ruled England from 1327 to 1377 and with his son, Edward the Black Prince, formed the Knights Order of the Garter and defeated the French at Crecy and Poitiers. At the feet of the suit of armour, four year old Joshua and one year old Rhianna play amongst their toys.

Outside, Mike is chatting to a visitor in fluent German, learned during the 80s and early 90s when he was working as a winemaker in Germany. Returning to New Zealand in 1995, the Justs decided to settle in Marlborough where Mike worked first for Merlen winery and then for eight years at Lawson's Dry Hills.

"Then in 2004 things really got going," says Paula, laughing and nodding towards the two children. "We started a family, moved up here to live and started making our own wine, all at the same time."

Inspired by the many great hillside vineyards they had seen in Europe, Mike and Paula had bought their 8 hectare plot high in the Omaka Valley and formed Clayridge Vineyards with family and friends in 1999. They planted 20,000 pinot noir vines, by hand. Unlike most on the low, flat plains of the region, these vines have never been irrigated, so they have established a natural deep rooting system that maximizes the potential of the unique terroir. Another vineyard, Escaroth Estate, (named after a town in Tolkein's The Hobbit), on a very similar site in the Taylor Valley, now grows exclusively for Clayridge using similar viticulture techniques.

"We started a family, moved up here to live and started making our own wine, all at the same time."

Mike is, not surprisingly, as adventurous in his winemaking as he is in his selection of vineyard sites. Hand picking, whole bunch pressing, wild fermentation, barrel maturation, and in the case of his Excalibur range, very small batches, are all features of his approach. He describes the resulting wines, sauvignon blanc and pinot noir, pinot blanc, pinot gris and riesling, as having lots of personality, character and individuality, which is exactly how people might describe Mike. Like winemaker, like wine.

Clayridge Vineyards

www.clayridgewines.co.nz

PO Box 51, Blenheim 7240
T + 64 3 577 8614
wines@clayridge.co.nz

Owned by
Mike & Paula Just

Brand
Clayridge

Varieties Pinot Blanc, Pinot Gris, Pinot Noir, Riesling, Sauvignon Blanc, Gewürztraminer, Viognier

Sub-region
Southern Valleys

Fighting the bugs with natural technology

At Rock Ferry, on the Wairau River, early settlers found a safe river crossing and now Tom Hutchison and Fiona Harvey have found a beautiful old property, the perfect escape from busy lives. There is something inspirational about the atmosphere and although his vineyard is some distance away, Tom feels a strong connection between how he feels when he spends time here and the way he feels about his wines.

Out in the Corners vineyard on Hammerichs Road, good progress is being made towards the achievement of full accreditation for the vineyard's organic practices, under the direction of viticultural consultant Bart Arnst. Tom says that the move to organic growing is about innovation, being ahead of the game. "It's definitely not the neatest vineyard you'll see," jokes Bart, waving a hand at what to some might look like weeds between the vines, "but there's

nothing accidental about the way we organise nature to do its best for us."

Originally planted in the early 1980s, the Corners has been progressively redeveloped since Tom purchased it in 1994. Its marvellous position, amongst the ancient river channels of the Wairau River, provides an ideal grape growing soil profile and varieties and clones suited to the site have been planted, namely pinot gris, sauvignon blanc, chardonnay, riesling and pinot blanc.

Winemaker Allan McWilliams lends his talents to crafting the wines using a combination of traditional and modern vinification methods. Hand picked fruit, whole bunch pressing, barrel fermentation and the use of cultured and indigenous yeasts reveal the inherent aromas and fruit weight of each grape variety and add complexity and texture to wines that are age-worthy and made to enjoy with food.

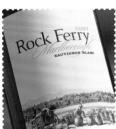

Rock Ferry Wines

www.rockferrywines.com

PO Box 544, Blenheim 7240
T + 64 3 577 6279
wine@rockferry.co.nz

Owned by
Tom Hutchison

Brand
Rock Ferry

Varieties Sauvignon Blanc, Pinot Gris, Chardonnay, Riesling, Pinot Blanc

Sub-region
Wairau

French connections

Off the coast of Madagascar is the French island of Reunion. One million people live on the island, which is not much larger than Marlborough, with its population of just 44,000. So there were plenty of changes to get used to for Georges and Huguette Michel and their teenage children when they moved from the heat of their Indian Ocean home to the variable climate of Marlborough in 1997.

Georges, who had previously owned a wine estate in Beaujolais/Burgundy, was keen to have a hands-on involvement in his new wine venture. Free from the strict traditions of European wine growing, he could decide exactly how things would be done.

Domaine Georges Michel, (*domaine* is French for wine estate), is situated in the Golden Mile area of the Wairau Valley, a micro terroir with a reputation for producing fine fruit and intense flavours. The first sauvignon blanc was released in 1998 followed by an oak-aged chardonnay and a pinot noir.

In 2003, just seven years after first stepping onto Marlborough soil, Georges and Huguette's daughter Swan joined the winemaking team after studying oenology at Lincoln University. "I have had a marvellous start to my wine career," says Swan. "After my degree I worked in France for Patrick Valette at Chateau le Grand Verdu and our old family friend, the winemaker Guy Brac de la Perrier, is my very special mentor."

Georges Michel is justly proud of his family's achievements and the success of his wines, and Marlborough is the richer for the Michel's decision to swap the tropics for this rather different style of paradise.

Domaine Georges Michel
....
www.georgesmichel.co.nz

56 Vintage Lane,
RD3, Blenheim 7273
T + 64 3 572 7230
sales@georgesmichel.co.nz

Owned by Georges Michel

Brand
Domaine Georges Michel

Varieties
Sauvignon Blanc,
Chardonnay, Pinot Noir,
Syrah, Viognier

Sub-region
Wairau

Visit
56 Vintage Lane,
Rapaura, Blenheim

• Cellar door
• Gourmet and gift shop
• La Veranda Vineyard
  Restaurant
• Winery tours by
  arrangement

A sparkling success

When Shin Yokoi and Tom Tenuwera bought Highfield in 1991, they came with some very useful connections. As the sole agent for Champagne Drappier in Japan, Shin knew one of the oldest French winemaking families. The new owners of Highfield were determined to make a name for their wines world-wide, but he and Tom were Champagne fans and keen to have a new world cuvée brut as their flagship wine. Hence,

Michel Drappier's help was enlisted and the first release of Elstree Cuvée Brut in 1993, like all those that followed, was a great success.

Since then, Elstree has remained a cornerstone of Highfield's reputation, which has been built under the direction of Alistair Soper (below), winemaker since 1999. Here's a man who believes in the value of standards. He's known for consistency of wine quality and style, and even

he would admit he's known for being picky. "We use sustainable vineyard practices, focusing on soil health. We respect the fruit at every stage. We hand pick for the Elstree. For the sauvignon blanc we don't even press, we only use free run juice. The second unusual thing we do with the sauvignon is let it sit on the yeast lees for four months. That gives the wine a rich, weighty mouth feel, which makes it superb with food."

Looking out from the landmark tower of

We respect the fruit at every stage. We hand pick for the Elstree. For the sauvignon blanc we don't even press, we only use free run juice.

the winery, across the Highfield vineyards planted on paddocks that once grazed sheep and horses, you can see the boundaries of Highfield Estate. Limited production keeps Highfield a boutique wine company. As well as the cuvée brut, the pinot noir, chardonnay, sauvignon blanc and riesling all feature in top restaurants and wine merchants around the world and attract the favourable attention of wine award judges and critics.

When asked whether he enjoys his job, Alistair grins. "Except when I'm angsting about frost, or too much rain at the wrong time, I'm like the cat with the cream. I am very fortunate to work for owners who are wine aficionados. They want me and my team to produce the very best wines we can. Quality matters as much to them as it does to all of us working in the vineyard and in the winery."

Highfield Estate
....
www.highfield.co.nz

Brookby Road,
RD2, Blenheim 7272
T + 64 3 572 9244
info@highfield.co.nz

Owned by
Shin Yokoi & Tom Tenuwera

Brands
Highfield, Elstree

Varieties
Sauvignon Blanc, Riesling,
Chardonnay, Pinot Noir

Sub-regions
Wairau, Southern Valleys

SWNZ accredited vineyard(s)
SWNZ accredited winery

Visit
Brookby Road, Blenheim

- Cellar door
- Winery tours by arrangement
- Highfield Restaurant
- Tower
- Art exhibitions

The House in the Sun

Anna Flowerday is a winemaker, born and brought up in McLaren Vale, South Australia. Jason Flowerday is also a winemaker and like Anna, he's from a grape-growing family, but as he says himself, he just can't compete with his wife's wine industry lineage which goes back five generations. The couple met at Hardys Tintara winery in Australia where they worked together, later branching out to own and run their own vineyard in the Clare Valley.

Still in their twenties, Anna and Jason decided that big dreams should not wait. They wanted their own wine company and they wanted to start a family too. So the search began for a solution, which presented itself in Marlborough, at Te Whare Ra, which translates from Māori as 'The House in the Sun'. "The name was legendary and although the place was run down it had great potential. We were raring to go," says Anna. "It was so good to be breathing new life into an icon of Marlborough's history," says Jason.

The pair rationalised the vineyard, planted new vines and renovated the house and winery. Somewhere along the way twins Sophie and Emily were born and babies in tow, vines were tended, grapes picked, wines made and awards collected. Te Whare Ra gewürztraminer has been the stand out. Then twins Charlotte and Isabel arrived to complete the dream.

The home vineyard is divided into three blocks, the oldest of which dates back to 1979. gewürztraminer, chardonnay, riesling, pinot gris, pinot noir, syrah and sauvignon blanc vines are tended with care using organic and biodynamic practices, helped by a small herd of manure-providing cows and a steer called Jack.

Having their own vineyard and winery and keeping production levels low means that Anna and Jason can do things exactly as they want to, staying true to their traditional winemaking values. When they need extra hands they call on friends and family. Whatever new dreams are on the Flowerday's horizon, Anna and Jason look all set to achieve them.

Te Whare Ra
....
www.tewharera.co.nz

PO Box 70, Renwick 7243
T + 64 3 572 8581
tewharera@xtra.co.nz

Owned by
The Flowerday Family

Brand
Te Whare Ra

Varieties
Gewürztraminer, Sauvignon Blanc, Riesling, Chardonnay, Pinot Gris, Pinot Noir, Syrah

Sub-regions
Wairau, Awatere

Visit
56 Anglesea Street, Renwick

• Cellar door
• Winery and vineyard tours by arrangement

A taste for detail

Ruud Maasdam and Dorien Vermaas started their wine business in the late 1990s and called it Staete Landt, the name given to New Zealand by the 17th century Dutch voyager Abel Tasman.

"We decided to make only single vineyard, estate grown wines which means that life has been a challenge at times," says Dorien. "After the frosts in 2003 for example, we lost 70% of the grapes, so we had very little wine to sell, but we didn't buy elsewhere. We're not prepared to compromise on our dream of what wine making should be about."

These days Ruud and Dorien spend weeks of each year travelling the world, extending their networks and meeting their customers at some of the world's top restaurants. Staete Landt's wines are selected by sommeliers in 18 countries with Denmark, Sweden and Finland looking likely to bring that number up to 21 very soon. That's one country for every hectare of the Staete Landt vineyard.

The old riverbed gravel soils of the Wairau River are planted in sauvignon blanc, chardonnay and pinot noir with smaller quantities of pinot gris, riesling, viognier and syrah. The vineyard, managed by viticulturist Charles Halliday (pictured left of Ruud and Dorien and one of their daughters, Annabel), is divided into 18 different blocks each with its own combination of clone, rootstock, soil type and viticulture regime. This arrangement offers Ruud an enormous diversity of flavour to work with in the winery where the juices from the different blocks are meticulously blended to produce specific characteristics in the wines.

"Our wines are made to go with food. Big on texture and complexity, and bone dry. We have in mind a certain type of wine drinker, someone who loves wine and knows a lot about it," says Ruud.

Most of those wines are bottled under cork. "To me wine is more voluptuous, more layered, more honest, under cork," says Ruud. "We're now one of the few New Zealand wine companies bottling mainly under cork and we're very proud of that."

Staete Landt

www.staetelandt.co.nz

PO Box 358, Blenheim 7240
T + 64 3 572 9006
wine@staetelandt.co.nz

Owned by
Ruud Maasdam &
Dorien Vermaas

Brand Staete Landt

Varieties
Sauvignon Blanc, Riesling, Chardonnay, Viognier,
Pinot Gris, Pinot Noir, Syrah

Sub-region Wairau

SWNZ accredited vineyard(s)

These secrets are state

When owners Bryan and Jan Johnson established their vineyard in the lower Waihopai Valley, the family were new to the wine industry. It was 1992 and many would have considered the ground here too dry, the climate too cold and the soils too poor for viticulture. But the Johnsons' intuition was sound and theirs has since become one of Marlborough's finest cool climate vineyards.

The quality of the wine is the most important element in Spy Valley's success but modern design and the clever, edgy humour of the brand conveys the new world thinking at the heart of the company.

When the move was made in 2000 from just growing grapes on Johnson Estate to producing their own wines, Bryan and Jan's daughter Amanda came up with the off-beat brand name. Spy Valley is what the locals call the valley, which is home not only to vineyards, but also to an international communications monitoring station with sinister-looking white satellite orbs.

"We were never going to be a run of the mill wine business," says Blair Gibbs, Amanda's husband and general manager of the company. "We essentially had a clean slate and we wanted to do things differently, to have fun with the brand. To their credit, Bryan and Jan have given us free rein to do that. Although," he adds, laughing, "maybe things would have been different if we

of the art

"We were never going to be a run of the mill wine business"

hadn't succeeded."

The Spy Valley brand might now be known throughout the world, but the company remains boutique in nature, and family-owned. Whilst having huge respect for the pioneers of Marlborough wine and the long established brands that first made the region's name, Blair and his team enjoy their newness and feel uninhibited about breaking new ground.

The most dramatic statement of the company's vision is its winery, one of

New Zealand's most advanced winemaking facilities. Set amongst the vines, in sympathy with its surroundings, the complex is testament to collaboration between winemakers, architects, planners and engineers and recently won the New Zealand Architects' Institute Supreme Commercial award.

Blair sees the Spy Valley label moving ahead with confidence, supported by continuing innovation, environmentally sound practices and a continuing quest to be the best.

Spy Valley Wines

www.spyvalleywine.co.nz

37 Lake Timara Road,
RD6, Blenheim 7276
T + 64 3 572 9840
info@spyvalley.co.nz

Owned by
Bryan & Jan Johnson

Brands Spy Valley, Envoy, Johnson Estate

Varieties Sauvignon Blanc, Riesling, Pinot Gris, Gewürztraminer, Chardonnay, Pinot Noir, Merlot

Sub-regions
Wairau, Southern Valleys

SWNZ accredited vineyard(s)
SWNZ accredited winery

Visit
37 Lake Timara Road,
Blenheim

• Cellar door
• Function venue

The will to succeed

Imagine looking down from a plane and picking a spot on the ground that is going to be your future. That's just about what Michael Tiller (above) did. As an Air New Zealand pilot he often flew into Blenheim airport and realised over time that one particular parcel of land, on a north facing slope of the Wairau Valley, seemed to be frost free even on the chilliest mornings. Michael and his family live and work on that land now and thankfully, they very rarely have to worry about frost.

At first, Michael and Robyn Tiller grew grapes for prominent Marlborough wine companies. But in the 1990s, with children growing up and more time to concentrate on the business, the Tillers decided to try their hands at making their own wines. Short of space, the venture had to get going in the tractor shed, but that didn't stop their first vintage being released to great acclaim.

Michael's mother, who passed away in 1983, would have been proud, and since those days, the wine estate named after her has grown without losing any of its focus. The Isabel range is estate grown, crafted and bottled, giving Michael and Robyn the luxury of having complete control over quality. High-density planting, low yields, organic viticulture practices, minimal irrigation and traditional hand harvesting reflect the Tiller's fierce respect for the grapes that need only the

> Clear vision and gritty determination characterises the Tiller approach to wine, work and life in general.

slightest coaxing to become wines worthy of their label.

Clear vision and gritty determination characterise the Tiller approach to wine, work and life in general. The children tell of Dad's single-mindedness when smitten by a particular car while on a visit to Canada. Though not exactly straightforward to ship, once seen, nothing was going to stop that little beauty getting a new home in Marlborough!

"We hope we've passed that kind of determination on to our offspring," says Robyn, laughing with Jane, Luke, Brad and Caitlin who all work in the vineyard and the winery, alongside the extended family of staff.

"Other people thought we were mad when we started," says Michael, "but we learned fast and we've had a ball. We have some great people working here and together we've made some very good wine. What more could we ask?"

Isabel Estate Vineyard

www.isabelestate.com

PO Box 29, Renwick 7243
T + 64 3 572 8300
info@isabelestate.com

Owned by
Michael & Robyn Tiller

Brand
Isabel

Varieties
Sauvignon Blanc, Pinot Noir,
Chardonnay, Pinot Gris,
Riesling

Sub-region
Wairau

Visit
70-72 Hawkesbury Road,
Renwick

- Cellar door
- Winery tours by arrangement
- Vineyard lodge accommodation

First vines, first wines

Croatian immigrant Ivan Yukich planted his first vines in the Waitakere Ranges west of Auckland in 1934. He sold his first wine in 1944. By the 1960s, Ivan's sons, Mate and Frank, had joined the business. They set up a company called Montana Wines and begun to expand into other areas. In 1973, Montana came to Marlborough, almost exactly a century after the region's first wine grower, David Herd, had planted his vineyard at Auntsfield.

Montana quietly bought land and started planting the first commercial vines in the region and four years later built the first commercial winery. From there the company went from strength to strength, changing hands along the way, until today it has the most extensive vineyard holdings and the largest winery in the region.

National wineries manager Gerry Gregg, has worked for Montana since the company first saw the potential for Marlborough sauvignon blanc. He was awarded the inaugural David Herd Lifetime Achievement Award in recognition of his contribution to the region's wine industry. As David Herd has become, Gerry is already something of a legend. There is a wine industry joke that everything at Montana is 'Gerry built'. He's amused and admits proudly that the place does

bear his mark. "Things have changed a good deal in all that time and I've seen flood, drought, frost, fire and international mergers. But it's all been worth it to see the winery become what it is today."

And what it is today is a massive complex on the main road into Blenheim from the south. Winery, wine education facility, restaurant, shop and cellar door of lofty proportions are all contained within a grand building reminiscent of a European chateau. The centre is known as the Montana Brancott Winery after the company's first vineyard in the Brancott Valley where the Marlborough Wine Festival is now held every year.

That original vineyard was planted in sauvignon blanc, the region's signature variety. But here, and in new vineyards in the Renwick area, pinot gris, riesling and pinot noir have been added.

Thousands of people have their first introduction to the art of making wine at Brancott. On the wine tour they are taken through each step of the process and meet Montana winemaker Patrick Materman (right) who has been responsible for Montana's Marlborough wines since 1994, or one of his team. Patrick tells visitors the story of sauvignon blanc and the other varieties and shares his enthusiasm for the region's newest success,

Montana Brancott Winery
. . . .
www.montana.co.nz
PO Box 331, Blenheim 7240
T + 64 3 578 2099
information@montana.co.nz

Owned by
Pernod Ricard New Zealand

Brand Montana

Varieties
Sauvignon Blanc, Pinot Gris, Riesling, Pinot Noir

Sub-regions Wairau, Southern Valleys

SWNZ accredited vineyard(s)
SWNZ accredited winery

Visit
State Highway 1, Riverlands, Blenheim

• Cellar door
• Winery tours
• Restaurant
• Private function rooms
• Event venue

"I like de-mystifying what we do. For many people, the idea that grapes pick up the personality of the soils they grow in is a revelation."

pinot noir. "I like de-mystifying what we do. For many people, the idea that grapes pick up the personality of the soils they grow in is a revelation," says Patrick. "They start to understand why wines taste different depending on where the grapes were grown, the season, and the winemaker. In the future they will be much more discerning wine buyers, and enjoy their wine more."

Montana is now owned by Pernod Ricard New Zealand giving the company enormous marketing reach and the name is known to wine buyers in just about every wine drinking corner of the globe. It is also associated with two of New Zealand's major arts events, the Montana World of Wearable Art Awards and the Montana Book Awards.

The locals scratched their heads in wonder when those Aucklanders starting planting vines all those years ago. Little did they think that not only would the idea work, but that more than 30 years on, the name Montana would still be around and Marlborough would be a world famous wine region.

A sense of place

As you head from Blenheim towards the Awatere Valley, before you reach Mount Riley's dry, hot and stony Seventeen Valley vineyard, you pass their winery planted amongst their Riverlands vines. The rows of vines intersect with a series of buildings that reflect the philosophy brought to each glass of wine by John Buchanan, daughter and sales and marketing director Amy, and winemaker son-in-law Matt Murphy (all pictured right).

The winery buildings, with their floor to ceiling windows, reveal the region's land and light beyond. This clarity and purity is what Mount Riley tries to capture in their wines. "It's our own down to earth translation of the French *terroir* – being faithful to the land, the climate and the fruit, allowing the vines, and the earth they grow in, their fullest, most honest expression," explains John.

Sauvignon blanc was Mount Riley's firstborn, planted in the 1980s, shortly after John bought what was the first of six vineyards that now spread their vines across the Wairau sub-region. "With our savvys we do our best to translate the wonderful fruit flavours and pour them straight into the bottle," says Matt.

Not content to leave it there, Mount Riley produce Marlborough's only traditional method sparkling sauvignon blanc. This wine was first enjoyed by the Buchanan family to celebrate the millennium and visitors to Mount Riley's cellar door are welcomed with a glass of this exuberant wine.

The secret ingredient in Mount Riley's recipe for success is people. "We enjoy the luxury of the best technology, but it's our people who illuminate our fruit's potential through hands-on attention to detail," says John. Amy adds that the relationship they have with their vines extends to all the people who work with them. "It's about family really, and that family includes our land, our people and, we'd like to think, our visitors and customers."

When you visit Mount Riley's winery and cellar door, you are standing on land that is close to the heart of the Mount Riley family. It is where John takes his grandsons for tractor rides, where winery dog Ruby and winery cat Tosca play hide and seek among the vines, and where Matt and Amy married in 2008. "We make our wines to celebrate such moments of kinship," says Amy. "We want our wine drinkers to taste that as they share the same kinds of moments in their own lives."

MOUNT RILEY

Mount Riley
www.mountriley.co.nz

10 Malthouse Road,
Riverlands, RD4,
Blenheim 7274
T + 64 3 577 9900
info@mountriley.co.nz

Owned by
John, Lyn & Amy Buchanan

Brand
Mount Riley

Varieties
Sauvignon Blanc,
Riesling, Chardonnay,
Pinot Gris, Pinot Noir,
Merlot Malbec

Sub-regions
Wairau, Southern Valleys

Visit
10 Malthouse Road,
Riverlands, Blenheim

• Cellar door
• Picnic area
• Pétanque court
• Display of photographs
  by Marti Friedlander

Birds of a feather

The huia bird, which is believed to have become extinct in the early 1900s, was sacred to Māori who wore its feathers, and much admired by Europeans for its beauty and uniquely different male and female bills. To this day the huia, with its glossy, blue-black, white tipped plumage and bright orange wattles, holds a special place in New Zealand's iconography.

To Mike and Claire Allan (right), the huia feather, with its connotations of strength, uniqueness, and attachment to this Pacific island, seemed the ideal symbol to sum up their hopes and dreams for the wine company they launched in 1996.

Claire, originally from Canterbury, came to the wine business via the hospitality industry. "After school I worked in restaurants, first front of house, then working my way up in the kitchen. I started to develop an interest in wine so I took off for Australia to study it." Mike, from Hawke's Bay, tried law, building and furniture-making before deciding on a career in wine.

When Mike and Claire bought a neglected orchard in Marlborough's Wairau Valley, 1.6 hectares of apples had to come out to make way for vines. But the Allans have taken a rather different approach to many growers, keeping most of the fruit and nut trees that had been on the property for generations. Olives, walnuts, almonds, apricots, citrus fruits and cherries all provide bounty for the family table and they have even planted apples to replace those they removed. And whatever they are growing, it is done with the future in mind, using sustainable practices. The business has achieved carboNZero® status.

Huia now has 32 hectares of its own vineyards and also sources grapes from a few dedicated growers from specific sites in the valley. "We want to keep the small business feel and to enjoy the life it gives us and our children. And we want to stay involved in the day to day work of managing the vineyards and producing wine," says Mike.

Most of Huia's production, including brut, pinot noir, chardonnay, pinot gris, gewürztraminer and sauvignon blanc, is snapped up by buyers in North America, Europe, Asia and Australia. Mike and Claire like to think that when their wines are winging their way to customers overseas, they are like huia birds, carrying a little of New Zealand with them.

Huia
....
www.huia.net.nz
PO Box 92,
Renwick 7243
T + 64 3 572 8326
wine@huia.net.nz

Owned by
Huia Vineyards Ltd

Brand Huia

Varieties Sauvignon Blanc, Riesling, Pinot Gris, Gewürztraminer, Chardonnay, Pinot Noir

Sub-regions
Wairau, Southern Valleys

SWNZ accredited vineyard(s)
SWNZ accredited winery
Certified carboNZero®

Visit
22 Boyces Road, Blenheim

• Cellar door
• Winery tours by arrangement

One man's wasteland is another man's vineyard

In the old days, very little grew on the stony river flats of the Wairau Valley. Farmers with enough patience might clear a block, painstakingly removing all the stones to reveal some meagre grazing for a few sheep. Who would have thought that one day the land would be so highly prized by a new breed of farmers, viticulturists like Stoneleigh's Rod Brailsford (far right). "Grapes do well in this environment. We planted sauvignon blanc and riesling vines first. Then we added chardonnay, merlot, pinot noir and pinot gris and they are just as happy."

The riverbed soils and the micro-climate in this Rapaura area, which is a little warmer than elsewhere in the region, combine to provide excellent grape growing conditions. The smooth river stones that litter the vineyard are not just tolerated but put to positive use. As well as

The smooth river stones that litter the vineyard are not just tolerated but put to positive use. As well as deterring weeds, they act as a heat sink.

deterring weeds, they act as a heat sink. They absorb the heat from the sun and reflect it back up onto the vines during the day, speeding up the ripening.

Out in the vineyard with Rod is Stoneleigh's winemaker, Jamie Marfell (far left). "Like every other vineyard, the grapes from ours reflect what's going on in this particular soil, the weather and how we manage those elements. My team and I then have the job of capitalising on all of that, bringing out the intense fruit flavours and texture that we get from this place, to produce wines that stand out as distinctly Stoneleigh." Born and raised locally, Jamie grew up with grapes and although he has worked overseas, he is a Marlborough man at heart. "Doesn't matter where you go, our sauvignon blanc is up there with the best and I love being part of that success."

Stoneleigh

www.stoneleigh.co.nz
Private Bag 92030,
Auckland 1148
T + 64 9 336 8300
information@stoneleigh.co.nz

Owned by
Pernod Ricard New Zealand

Brand
Stoneleigh

Varieties Sauvignon Blanc, Chardonnay, Riesling, Pinot Gris, Pinot Grigio, Merlot, Pinot Noir

Sub-region Wairau

SWNZ accredited vineyard(s)

A Pom, an Aussie, a Kiwi... and the Portuguese connection

Dr Andrew Hedley, chief winemaker, says there is something about Framingham that makes people want to pitch in and do their best. He's not sure what it is, and much too modest in an English kind of way to suggest that it might just be him. Andrew has been a cornerstone of the business since joining the company in 2001, having moved to New Zealand from the north east of England just three years earlier. "We don't take ourselves too seriously, but the growing and winemaking process is a different matter."

Andrew's dry sense of humour is counterbalanced by viticulturist Anton Groffen's more ready wit, born of an upbringing in South Australia. The wine industry was an early career choice for Anton (left). He graduated in viticulture and a post-graduate scholarship at the Orlando Wyndham Group gave him an excellent grounding in the practical side of

"We don't take ourselves too seriously, but the growing and winemaking process is a different matter."

the job. He loves every minute of it.

Framingham is growing on a few other vineyards these days, but the home block boasts some of the oldest vines in Marlborough. It was planted by Rex Brooke-Taylor, the founder of Framingham, who showed foresight and persistence with aromatic wines at a time when he was under pressure to remove the vines and replant with other varieties. Tom Trolove, general manager and proud Marlburian, says that it's this heritage that has provided the foundation for Framingham's current focus on aromatic varieties, "The vine age plays a key role in the unique quality of our wines."

Framingham produced its first wine in 1994, leading off with rieslings that received excellent reviews, sold well and set the pace for future years. In 1998 a winery was built and over the years the range has expanded to include sauvignon blanc, pinot gris, gewürztraminer, chardonnay, montepulciano and pinot noir. "For me, riesling is quite an obsession," says Andrew. "We make four distinctly different styles, all from our own single estate vineyard. The vineyard is the star but it's up to Anton and me to make sure that it can shine."

And the Portuguese connection? Well Framingham is now owned by a Portuguese wine family. They have discovered a new world wine region that excites them and it's fair to say they already love Marlborough aromatic wines.

Framingham Wines

www.framingham.co.nz

PO Box 37, Renwick 7243
T + 64 3 572 8884
info@framingham.co.nz

Owned by
Sogrape

Brand Framingham

Varieties Sauvignon Blanc, Pinot Noir, Riesling, Pinot Gris, Chardonnay, Gewürztraminer, Montepulciano

Sub-regions
Wairau, Southern Valleys

SWNZ accredited vineyard(s)

Visit
19 Conders Bend Road, Renwick

• Cellar door
• Under ground cellars
• Rose garden
• Native garden
• Board room
• Accommodation

Whales, waves and wine

Kaikoura Winery, just outside Kaikoura township, is the most southern and quite possibly the most spectacular Marlborough winery location. Situated on a limestone bluff overlooking the Pacific Ocean, the views from here, in any kind of weather, just knock your socks off and blow you away. Out to sea the dolphins frolic and you can spot the whale-watching boats on the horizon. Inland, mountain peaks tower above the home vineyard, snow-capped for much of the year.

Kaikoura Winery was founded in 1999 by a direct descendant of Luke and Anne Abraham, the first Europeans to settle in the area. A vineyard was planted with pinot noir, chardonnay, pinot gris and gewürztraminer vines, and a trial block of sauvignon blanc established. Salty, and vulnerable to southerly blasts, this is challenging growing country and the vineyard has been kept small. Additional grapes for the Kaikoura wine range are sourced from other Marlborough growers.

The waters off this coastline are famous, not only for whale-watching, but also for their bounty of crayfish, sometimes called rock lobster. So it is fitting, and no surprise, that the company's flagship wine is a rosé that goes perfectly with seafood. The Estate Rosé is made exclusively from grapes grown in the Kaikoura district and made in the tiny home winery. The balance of the Kaikoura wine range is made at Marlborough's Lawson's Dry Hills winery.

There are natural limestone caves nearby and these provided the inspiration for the building of a very large underground cellar where wines can be aged at a stable temperature of 12°C.

The Kaikoura local authority is the first in the world to achieve Green Globe certification in recognition of its commitment to protecting the environment and working towards sustainability for residents, visitors and generations to come. "The winery likes to play its part," says Neroli Gold, part-owner of the winery and a strong supporter of the council's stand on environmental and sustainability issues. "So the cellar has hosted Eco Art events and our staff have made some ingenious outfits for Kaikoura's Trash to Fashion show from hundreds of corks and screw caps, drawing attention to our zero waste policy."

The team at Kaikoura Winery are serious about their wines, but they certainly know how to have fun. It must be something in that bracing sea air.

Kaikoura Winery

www.kaikourawinery.co.nz

PO Box 11, Kaikoura 7340
T + 64 3 319 7966
info@kaikourawinery.co.nz

Owned by
Kaikoura Wine Company

Brand
Kaikoura

Varieties Chardonnay, Sauvignon Blanc, Riesling, Gewürztraminer, Pinot Noir

Sub-regions
Wairau, Kaikoura

Visit
140 State Highway 1,
2kms south of Kaikoura

- Cellar door
- Winery tour every hour
- Kaikoura Winery Café
- Art exhibitions
- Wedding and function venue

Home grown talent

Kathy Lynskey is very much the local girl. Raised in Havelock on the family farm, she was brought up to be competent, capable and with a can-do attitude.

Taking off to Australia in the 1980s, Kathy spent time in the Hunter and Barossa valleys, regions already well known for their wines and way ahead of the Marlborough wine industry which was still in its infancy. In 1989 she returned home to Marlborough armed with enthusiasm and ambition and promptly bought a vineyard, becoming one of the first women in the area to undertake such a development alone. "A natural affinity with the land, a love of wine and a strong will to succeed were my three vital ingredients," says Kathy, recalling those early days when she planted most of the vineyard by herself.

Although she had decided that she would make great wines of her own one day, Kathy concentrated on the vineyard and grew for other wine companies until 1998 when a different block of land was bought and developed. The Lynskeys Wairau Peaks label was launched, later to become simply Kathy Lynskey Wines. The range includes gewürztraminer, pinot noir, merlot, chardonnay,

sauvignon blanc and pinot gris.

Today, Kathy and her Californian-born partner, Kent Casto, hand craft their range of single vineyard and reserve wines under the guidance of respected winemaker Alan McCorkindale. Their wines gather awards and accolades, particularly in the United States which is the major export market for the brand.

Wine is Kathy's lifelong passion, but she has another too – gardening. "I just love my roses. My favourite finish to the day is a stroll in the garden with Kent and the cats, enjoying a glass of wine and appreciating all that we have achieved."

Kathy Lynskey Wines

www.kathylynskeywines.co.nz
PO Box 874, Blenheim 7240
T + 64 3 579 5696
lynskeys.wines@xtra.co.nz

Owned by
Kathy Lynskey & Kent Casto

Brand
Kathy Lynskey Wines

Varieties
Pinot Noir, Merlot, Gewürztraminer, Chardonnay, Sauvignon Blanc, Pinot Gris

Sub-region Wairau

Vineyard ahoy!

Immersed in the frenzied world of finance in 1980s Wellington, Greg and Sue White decided to make a radical lifestyle change. Shedding their business suits, they went sailing, first to the Pacific Islands and then around the New Zealand coast, eventually dropping anchor in the Marlborough Sounds.

Greg's financial skills, Sue's optimism and energy and Simon's winemaking expertise proved a winning combination.

A visit ashore lured them into their next great adventure. Sampling a glass or two of Marlborough sauvignon blanc prompted them to think that growing a few grapes might be just the sort of project to bring them back to dry land. This was 1994, when Marlborough's wineries could still be counted on a couple of hands.

Despite a lack of viticulture skills, or any experience with the soil, the Whites took over the lease of a wine company, lock, stock and barrel and were fortunate to land the services of a talented winemaker from Gisborne, Simon Waghorn.

Greg's financial skills, Sue's optimism and energy and Simon's winemaking expertise proved a winning combination. Together they built a name for their dream, the Whitehaven Wine Company, which in very short order was exporting over 200,000 cases a year to the United Kingdom, Ireland, Japan, Hong Kong, Australia and increasingly, to North America.

Using grapes from Whitehaven's own 16 hectares of vineyards, and from 30 contract growers, from sites across Marlborough's Wairau and Awatere Valleys, Whitehaven is in the fortunate position of having the whole spectrum of fruit characters from which to select grapes. Whitehaven produces the full range of Marlborough whites, but is also committed to pinot noir, anticipating increasing interest in Marlborough's success with this variety.

Greg and Sue never did go back to life at sea but what had proved to be a 13-year romantic adventure for a pair of fugitives from the city drew to a close early in 2007 when Greg passed away. Today, Sue, winemaker Simon, and a committed team, carry on the dream. They continue to focus on creating wines with the authentic Marlborough flavours and qualities that have helped to build Whitehaven's reputation.

Whitehaven Wine Company

....

www.whitehaven.co.nz

39 Pauls Road, Rapaura,
RD3, Blenheim 7273
T + 64 3 572 7588
info@whitehaven.co.nz

Owned by The White Family
& associates

Brands
Whitehaven, Mansion House Bay,
Whites Bay, Whitecaps

Varieties
Sauvignon Blanc, Chardonnay,
Pinot Gris, Riesling,
Gewürztraminer, Pinot Noir

Sub-regions
Wairau, Awatere, Southern Valleys

Visit
1 Dodson Street,
Blenheim

• Cellar door
• Conservatory
  Restaurant

Escaping the rat race

Nev Gane, Mud House's vineyard manager in Marlborough, takes us right up to the top of the hill so that we can look out over the 100 hectares that is the Mud House Marlborough vineyard. The view is spectacular. "Not a bad place to work," says Nev looking pleased as punch with his lot.

Nev doesn't take this landscape for granted, but it is his native habitat. By contrast his bosses come from urban backgrounds with earlier careers doing high powered corporate things in big cities. All successful in former ventures, they are to a man escapees from the rat race, happy to now be steering one of New Zealand's younger but larger wine industry players, and living in the South Island.

These people see the wine business from the sharp end, through a glass, having been sampling the stuff for over three quarters of a century between them, in the best restaurants in the world. "Most wine companies are led by grape growers or winemakers. Mud House is a wine drinkers' winery," says CEO Baden Ngan-Kee who is quick to add that

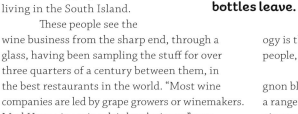

Right first time, every time ... this discipline runs through the whole process from the moment the grapes arrive to the time the labelled bottles leave.

he is only joking, because in the end it is the winemakers who make the company's reputation.

Back on the hill, the big yellow harvesters are zig-zagging across the blanket of green. At the winery it is all systems go. Right first time, every time, is a fine corporate mantra that has its place in wine businesses, as in any other. This discipline runs through the whole process from the moment the grapes arrive to the time the labelled bottles leave.

Ant Mackenzie, chief winemaker, has worked at some pretty impressive wineries, overseas and in New Zealand, and he is thoroughly enjoying this one. "Having great grapes is the first thing and having the best available technology is the second. The third element for me is the people, and this team is just fantastic."

In Marlborough, Mud House makes sauvignon blanc, chardonnay, pinot noir and merlot in a range of styles and continues to search for new vineyards in the region to enhance the winemaking options. Nev and his team will be kept busy.

Mud House Wines

www.mudhouse.co.nz

PO Box 91, Waipara 7447
T + 64 3 314 6900
wine@mudhouse.co.nz

Owned by
The MH Wine Group Ltd.

Brands
Mud House, Mud House Swan, Hay Maker

Varieties Sauvignon Blanc, Chardonnay, Pinot Noir

Sub-region
Southern Valleys

SWNZ accredited vineyard(s)

Nothing ventured, nothing gained

Blind River in the Awatere Valley. Traditionally this is sheep farming country but the potential for grape growing was recognised as far back as 1847 when Frederick Weld, an early settler who later became prime minister, wrote in his diary, "I intend having a garden and a vinery in a deep glen behind the house." But his vision was not realised until 153 years later when Murray and Daphne Brown became the first in the Blind River valley to convert farmland to vineyards.

The Browns have been immersed in winegrowing in the Marlborough region for decades. They planted some of the region's first grapes on the stony Rapaura soils and established the highly regarded Cairnbrae label. But Murray was drawn to the arid landscape of the Blind River area, south of Seddon, bought over 120 hectares and established a new venture. Named after a local headland, Cape Campbell Wines has

Water was always going to be an issue – the Browns and some neighbours formed the Blind River irrigation scheme including a dam which attracts all manner of wildlife.

taken as a logo the landmark's historic lighthouse symbolising the strong pioneering spirit of the area.

The move was a risky business. Cape Campbell attracts the weather off the Kaikoura ranges and pushes it out onto Cook Strait. While this ensures that the area misses most of the cold southerly weather moving up the country, it also means rainfall is low; less than half the precipitation of the Wairau Valley. Water was always going to be an issue. As a solution, the Browns and some innovative neighbours formed the Blind River irrigation scheme including a 3.6 hectare dam which attracts all manner of wildlife.

Such pioneering instinct underpinned the Brown's belief that despite the obstacles, great wines would be produced from this new region. Accolades for their sauvignon blanc, chardonnay, riesling, pinot gris, gewürztraminer and pinot noir, proved them right and are testament to the hard work, commitment and skill of the small, close-knit and very family orientated team.

The Brown's son Dion is now a director of the company, working with his parents. Lucy Weenink has been general manager for almost 10 years, and consultant Matt Thomson has worked alongside the Browns since Cairnbrae days becoming, in that time, one of New Zealand's leading winemakers.

Unusually, the clouds threaten rain as Murray and Daphne head out to check on the new plantings that are extending the vineyard to meet demand. The Cape Campbell story is still unfolding.

Cape Campbell Wines

www.capecampbell.co.nz
PO Box 5024, Springlands,
Blenheim 7241
T + 64 3 579 4250
wine@capecampbell.co.nz

Owned by
Murray & Daphne Brown

Brands
Cape Campbell, Cable Station, Blenheim Point

Varieties
Sauvignon Blanc, Chardonnay, Riesling, Pinot Gris, Pinot Noir, Gewürztraminer

Sub-region
Awatere

People who have been in the Marlborough wine business for as long as Philip and Janey Walsh are entitled to indulge in just a touch of self-satisfaction. They really are pioneers; they were growing grapes in 1975. Their wealth of experience, born of the good times and bad, just cannot be gained overnight, no matter how smart any new kid on the block might be. And it shows.

A thirty year apprenticeship

Over three decades, the Walshes planted, nurtured and improved their Dog Point Road property, turning 33 hectares of boulder strewn flats on the Omaka River into prime viticultural land. With the combined input of farmer and gardener, they created a meticulously managed vineyard producing high quality grapes that were sold to some of the best names in Marlborough.

Then, as the century turned, they decided that the time had come to take the plunge and establish their own label. They called it Bouldevines, simply because they have dealt with a lot of boulders over the years. Philip laughs, "My father spent years getting the stones off this land, backbreaking work. And now everyone's putting them all back, under the vines."

2005 was the first vintage of Bouldevines estate grown, single vineyard chardonnay and sauvignon blanc. Since then the brand has quickly become established with winemaker Drew Ellis producing medal winning wines that are being drunk in Singapore, Hong Kong, Australia and the United Kingdom, as well as closer to home. And Philip and Janey's son Jeremy has now joined the business.

"We will always feel very connected to the land which our families have farmed for generations," says Janey, "and we are happy now to be seeing the process right through to producing our own wines and seeing them doing well. It's a wonderful feeling."

Bouldevines Wines

....

www.bouldevineswine.co.nz

198 Dog Point Road, RD2,
Blenheim 7272
T + 64 3 572 8010
sales@bouldevineswine.co.nz

Owned by PJ & BJ Walsh

Brand
Bouldevines

Varieties Sauvignon Blanc,
Chardonnay, Riesling,
Pinot Gris, Gewürztraminer,
Pinot Noir

Sub-region Southern Valleys

SWNZ accredited vineyard(s)

Visit
The Wine Cellar at
The Vines Village,
193 Rapaura Road

• Cellar door
• Café

Wines of divine proportions

The nautilus is an ancient sea creature that adds chambers to its elaborate and beautiful shell as it grows. Like the nautilus, this wine company has steadily developed since its foundation in 1985 by Robert Hill Smith, fifth generation proprietor and vigneron of Australian wine company Yalumba.

Nautilus Estate is still in the ownership of the Hill Smith family and still growing. Early on, the label became widely admired for its bottle-fermented méthode traditionelle wine. Today the range includes sauvignon blanc, chardonnay, pinot gris and pinot noir.

Vineyards in the Wairau, Awatere and southern valleys, harness the sub-regional characteristics of the Marlborough terroirs. The viticultural team is focused on identifying and enhancing the key characteristics and unique qualities each of these sub-regional sites can bring to the wines.

The winemaking team, headed for over 10 years by Clive Jones, takes the bounty of these vineyards and works its magic using the best of modern and traditional winemaking techniques. They have the best of modern winemaking facilities to play with; two completely separate wineries for processing white wines and pinot noir, the latter facility being the first of its kind in the southern hemisphere.

Clive Jones likes the idea of his handiwork being represented by a nautilus shell on the wine label. Standing by the huge nautilus shell sculpture by Dale Hudson that marks the entrance to the company's cellar door and winery, Clive explains that the shell's construction proceeds in a logarithmic spiral and is said by mathematicians to have "divine proportions". He doesn't want to boast, but he thinks that fits very well with the wine he and the team produce year after year and that is now consumed in over 30 countries around the world.

Nautilus Estate of Marlborough

....

www.nautilusestate.com

PO Box 107, Renwick 7243
T + 64 3 579 6008
sales@nautilusestate.com

Owned by
Hill Smith Family

Brands
Nautilus, Opawa, Twin Islands

Varieties
Sauvignon Blanc, Pinot Noir, Pinot Gris, Chardonnay

Sub-regions Wairau, Awatere, Southern Valleys

SWNZ accredited vineyard(s)
SWNZ accredited winery.

Visit
12 Rapaura Road

- Cellar door
- Winery tours by arrangement
- Cheese platters

A Vine Life

On the edge of David Dew's newly acquired vineyard, the Omaka River babbles its way towards the Wairau Valley. "Having the river on the property is a real delight. I love rivers – to me they represent the flow of life, sometimes flowing fast over rapids, sometimes flowing more slowly through pools, but always moving. So choosing the name was easy."

Farming is in David's blood although a career in law has meant he hasn't had much dirt under his nails since his childhood. As a young man, David (above) left the family farm in rural Taranaki to study in Wellington and arrived in Marlborough in 1973 to join a Blenheim law firm. Given his background, he was interested in what was happening in the local farming community and was quick to notice that sheep farms were starting to sprout vines. With a few colleagues he decided to invest some money in the new crop and established what was amongst the first independent grape growing ventures in the region.

Over the years, David's interest in the wine industry developed until in 2008 he founded his own label. "In some ways I am a late starter, only now finding the time to get into making wine, but in other ways I'm a bit of a veteran having been involved in the Marlborough wine industry, through our vineyards and through my legal practice, since the beginning."

The three winery-owned vineyards, all located on the southern side of the Wairau Valley, have different soil structures, micro-climates and vine age, offering a range of fruit characteristics for River Farm's consultant winemaker, Brian Bicknell, to work with. David has already had the satisfaction of pouring the first glass of River Farm wine, the 2008 sauvignon blanc. "We're so pleased with it and very excited about adding wines to the range and gaining converts in New Zealand and overseas, not to mention opening our new cellar door," says David, looking very happy indeed with his move into the front-line of Marlborough's wine business.

River Farm Wines

www.riverfarmwines.co.nz

36 Godfrey Road,
RD2, Blenheim 7272
T +64 3 572 9091
info@riverfarmwines.co.nz

Owned by
River Farm Vineyards Ltd.

Brand
River Farm Wines

Varieties
Sauvignon Blanc, Merlot,
Pinot Noir, Pinot Gris

Sub-regions
Wairau, Southern Valleys

Visit
36 Godfrey Road,
Blenheim

• Cellar door

Rising through the ranks

Not far off 30 years ago, the going rate for pruning was less than three dollars an hour, but teenage brothers Mike and Paul Eaton were coining rather more than that having negotiated piece rates and figured out a way of getting the job done twice as fast as everyone else.

Mike's precocious talent for efficiency stayed with him, adding an extra edge to hands-on experience as he learned every aspect of the grape growing business from the bottom up. Nearly three decades later Mike, with his wife Jo, is the proud owner of TerraVin, a hillside vineyard on the clay-bound gravels of the Omaka Valley. They have made their name as pinot noir specialists.

Mike (right) believes in looking after the land that feeds him. He uses holistic practices in managing the vineyard. "With a bit of persuasion, nature will do a lot of work for you if you don't get in its way," says Mike, pointing out various species of flowers grown between the vines to attract beneficial insects and maintain soil nutrition.

The minimalist approach is taken into the winery too where Mike has developed his winemaking talents by working alongside some of the most adventurous winemakers in the region. Of a recent addition to the TerraVin range Mike says, "It was just a beautiful thing; hardly required any actual making after the work we had done in the vineyard, then hand picking, careful selection and nurturing the juice in oak."

This is the way Mike and Jo want to move forward, making smaller quantities of better and better wines. As his sons grow, he hopes they will inherit not only his love of wine but also his conviction that by thinking and working smart and respecting your raw materials, you can achieve what you want, and more.

TerraVin Wines

....

www.terravin.co.nz

367 Brookby Road,
RD2, Blenheim 7272
T + 64 3 572 9890
pinot@terravin.co.nz

Owned by Mike & Jo Eaton

Brand
TerraVin

Varieties
Pinot Noir, Sauvignon
Blanc, Chardonnay,
Cabernet Merlot/Malbec,
Pinot Gris

Sub-region
Southern Valleys

Visit
The Wine Cellar at
The Vines Village,
197 Rapaura Road,
Blenheim

• Cellar door

Going it alone

Most wine companies have vineyards. Some wine companies have their own wineries. But David Clouston is travelling light; he has neither a vineyard nor a winery.

David (above) learned his craft as a winemaker working over 20 vintages around the world and in New Zealand before taking the step of starting Two Rivers of Marlborough in 2004. "Over the years I came to the conclusion that I wanted to concentrate one hundred percent on my craft. I am a winemaker through and through and I don't want to be distracted by owning property or managing all the other bits of the process. I am interested in the other elements of the process, but at this stage my main focus is on making the best wine I can."

So David has scoured the Wairau and Awatere valleys to select his vines, not just vineyard by vineyard but row by row, being picky about soils, climate, orientation and all manner of other variables including the grower's viticulture philosophy. He has contracts with growers, to provide him with what he considers to be the highest quality sauvignon blanc, pinot gris, riesling and pinot noir grapes. "The growers like what I'm trying to do and we work well together."

Once the harvest is in and the grapes delivered to the winery where he camps out, he is pretty much his own chief cook and bottle washer. Traditionally, winemaking teams are very well looked after during the busy vintage period. "It's hard work, but you're spoiled a bit, you're fed at all hours of the day and night. Now I make my own sandwiches," says David.

So far, David's independent approach seems to be working. "I sold out in 2007 and I have orders from Europe for the '08 release so it is a very exciting time for Two Rivers of Marlborough."

Two Rivers of Marlborough

www.tworiversofmarlborough.co.nz

PO Box 5180, Springlands,
Blenheim 7241
T + 64 21 527 550
dave@tworiversofmarlborough.co.nz

Owned by David Clouston

Brand
Two Rivers of Marlborough

Varieties
Pinot Gris, Pinot Noir, Riesling, Sauvignon Blanc

Sub-regions
Wairau, Awatere

High ideals and a light touch

Not many teenagers know the difference between a Pouilly Fumé and a Pouilly Fuissé, but Sam Weaver did. At 16, he started working in the wine department of his local supermarket and so began a journey through the wine world that led him to settle in Marlborough. En route from Shropshire, England, Sam studied microbiology, worked as a fine wine merchant, made wine in France and became a winemaker and consultant in New Zealand, developing brands for many well-known companies.

Sam's blend of technical skill and experience, international market knowledge, palate-training and consumer insight is unusual and has fitted well with Mandy Weaver's business background to provide the company with a very firm foundation.

Tucked away in rolling hills 200 metres above sea level, the main Churton vineyard overlooks both the Omaka and Waihopai valleys. Here Sam and Mandy have created a European-style vineyard that has the advantage of a hillside aspect, with a soil structure that is free-draining but also retains water. With little or no irrigation, the close-planted vines are forced to work hard and compete with each other for moisture, sending their roots deep into the soil. The result is small crops of intensely flavoured fruit.

To produce grapes that meet his exacting standards, Sam believes in working closely with nature. Where possible, he applies biodynamic practices and strict yield control and is constantly making the smallest of adjustments in the vineyard to finely tune the end product.

The same uncompromising and disciplined approach is brought to bear in the winery where Sam crafts Churton's sauvignon blanc and pinot noir. "I am going for wines of length, texture and finesse, designed to flow across the palate and unfold in flavour towards the end. They're designed to be enjoyed with good food," says Sam, whose own palate received invaluable refinement when he was tasting two or three hundred international wines a week

To produce grapes that meet his exacting standards, Sam believes in working closely with nature.

as a London fine wine merchant.

Now Churton wines, named after Sam's birthplace, are being drunk throughout the world, including in the finer dining restaurants of Shropshire, where it all began.

Churton

www.churton-wines.co.nz

PO Box 25, Renwick 7243
Tel. +64 3 572 4007
info@churton-wines.co.nz

Owned by
Sam & Mandy Weaver

Brand Churton

Varieties Sauvignon Blanc, Pinot Noir

Sub-region Southern Valleys

SWNZ accredited vineyard(s)

Seriously good fun

The Ned vineyard and wine brand is taking shape and Brent Marris's vision is steadily being realised. "As a kid I spent countless hours hiking and biking in this area," says Brent. "From the summit of The Ned, one of the tallest, most rugged peaks around here, I could see the North Island and look out to the Pacific Ocean. I loved my childhood and when we were looking for a name for my new brand I wanted to celebrate my Marlborough heritage. The Ned says it all."

Brent has been making wine in Marlborough since 1990 but at a time when he might have been thinking about resting on his laurels, he began a search for a new, very special vineyard. Using his vast local knowledge he soon found just what he was looking for, 270 hectares tucked between the Delta hills and the Waihopai River. This area enjoys consistently cool nights, warmer daytime temperatures and lower rainfall than areas to the north. The property is now planted in sauvignon blanc and pinot gris with a separate pinot noir vineyard tucked into the hills to the east. The first wines from The Ned hit the streets in 2005.

As he walks along the river that runs the full length of the vineyard, talking about his plans, you can't miss Brent's absolute delight in his find. And you see quite clearly that this is a man on a mission. At this stage in his life and career, he wants to focus on quality. "With all the experience I've gained over the years and a property like this, I'm like a kid in a toy shop. I want to play." To win of course. The Marrises are a very competitive family.

His ambition on this virgin wine territory is to work with what nature has to offer, in harmony with the native flora, fauna and natural land formations. The vineyard buildings are partly concealed in a terrace bank, grass on top, busy operations yard below. Falcon breeding is encouraged, with nesting boxes and feeding stations provided for the resident pair in the hope that their population will increase. More falcons means less need for nets or noisy birdscarers to protect ripening fruit. The 120 million litre resevoir, which stores water for irrigation, is moulded into contours of the terrace and lined with river stones to create a refuge for local water fowl. The birds are occasionally surprised to find themselves observing a golf driving competition when Brent's family is around. The target is a bucket on a pontoon in the middle of the reservoir. The winner gets the job of rowing out in the dinghy to retrieve the balls.

Brent Marris loves to see his children playing here and although the family does not live on the property, it is home away from home. There is a long way to go before The Ned is everything Brent wants it to be, but he relishes the journey, which is taking him full circle, back to his roots.

The Ned

....

www.thened.co.nz

26 Arney Crescent,
Remuera, Auckland 1050
T + 64 9 522 9684
info@thened.co.nz

Owned by
Brent & Rosemary Marris

Brand
The Ned

Varieties
Sauvignon Blanc, Pinot Gris, Pinot Noir

Sub-region
Southern Valleys

"With all the experience I've gained over the years and a property like this, I'm like a kid in a toy shop."

A perfect landing in Marlborough

Robina and Geoff Jensen are very fond of the springs and the wetland area that captures everyone's attention as soon as they turn into the driveway to the winery. It has a rather otherworldly feel about it. The water is perfectly still, a little spooky but alluringly peaceful. At one time, before the settlers came farming, the whole region would have looked much like this. The peace is only broken by the frogs, croaking to each other.

The Jensens found this beautiful spot in the Wairau Valley when they were looking for an earthbound project having spent much of their lives up in the air, Geoff as a pilot and Robina as an airline purser. "In 1992 it still felt rather daring to be buying 20 odd hectares of land in Marlborough and hoping to make a living from grapes and olives. The industry had been going for nearly 20 years but compared to what has happened in the last 15, development had been quite slow," says Robina remembering her first vineyard nerves.

The original vineyard was planted mainly in sauvignon blanc with a small amount of semillon and merlot. Chardonnay and pinot noir came next. Not far away, on Falveys Road, an additional vineyard now grows more of the same varieties as well as pinot gris. Today, 72 hectares produce a crop weighing in at around 500 tonnes a year.

All the fruit is handled in the Omaka Springs on-site winery under the watchful eye of resident winemaker Ian Marchant (above), originally from the United Kingdom, but now very much at home in Marlborough.

The variety that stands out from the Omaka Springs list is semillon. "Ah, yes, that's our secret ingredient," says Geoff with a laugh before telling all. "We like to blend a little semillon with our sauvignon blanc to give it what our winemaker calls 'that extra twist of herbaceousness'."

There is another secret ingredient in Geoff and Robina's wines, and it comes from under the ground. The Omaka vines are irrigated with the pure waters of the springs and whatever it is that they bring to the surface, the grapes do exceedingly well on it.

"In 1992 it still felt rather daring to be buying 20 odd hectares of land in Marlborough and hoping to make a living from grapes and olives."

Omaka Springs Estates

www.omaka.co.nz

PO Box 39, Renwick 7243
T + 64 3 572 9933
wine@omaka.co.nz

Owned by
Geoff & Robina Jensen

Brand
Omaka Springs Estates

Varieties
Sauvignon Blanc, Pinot Gris, Riesling, Chardonnay, Semillon, Pinot Noir, Merlot

Sub-region
Southern Valleys

Visit
The Wine Room, SH1, 3kms north of Blenheim

- Cellar door
- Café
- Winery tours by arrangement

Rapaura visionaries

There's a life size corrugated iron cow standing on the lawn of the Wairau River restaurant. "The family have cursed me for buying that sculpture," says Chris Rose, "because it takes two or three people to move it in and out every day, but I love it. It fits the quirky way we do things."

Chris and Phil Rose have been doing things their own way for as long as anyone can remember. For all their success and their status as early pioneers of the Marlborough wine industry, Chris and Phil are as down to earth as ever, and disarmingly frank. "We do have control freak tendencies in this family," admits Phil, "but they are well-satisfied because we've always done everything ourselves, from growing the grapes to making the wine, bottling it and sending it to market."

The Roses say they owe much of their success to the quality of the region's natural resources so they work hard to look after the environment.

Chris and Phil were originally lucerne growers but with the bottom falling out of the market, they decided to try grape growing on their land on the banks of the Wairau River. Way back in the 1970s this was a bold step and easier said than done. Before they could plant their first vines, they had to go all the way to the High Court to overcome zoning regulations and 50 objections. They won their case and the Rose's vision and perseverance paved the way for further vineyard development in the Rapaura district which soon became known as Marlborough's 'golden mile'.

After more than a decade growing grapes on contract for local wineries, Chris and Phil decided to produce their own wines and since the first release of Wairau River wines in 1991 the label has continued to gain in strength and reputation.

Five vineyards, on over 200 hectares, provide all the fruit for the Wairau River range of sauvignon blanc, pinot gris, riesling, gewürztraminer, chardonnay and pinot noir. Today, exports to more than 10 countries account for around 80% of sales.

The Roses say they owe much of their success to the quality of the region's natural resources, so they work hard to look after the environment. They find ways to use natural solutions in the vineyard; restoring riverbanks, planting natives and using sustainable materials. They have recently put in a waste water cleaning and recycling system and are carboNZero® certified.

Wairau River Wines is a tight-knit family business. As the business grew, so did Chris and Phil's family. Now their five children are all involved, plus partners. Son-in-law Parky is general manager, daughter Pip (above, far right) runs the cellar door, son Hamish (driving harvester) is the viticulturist and Phil's right hand man. Son Sam is the winemaker. Daughter Anna helps out wherever needed and daughter Caroline and her partner Tane (above, second & third right) are chefs in the vineyard restaurant. "And when we run out of family we employ wonderful staff. They're our extended family," says Phil.

At lunch time, visitors are enjoying delicious food on the shady verandahs of the mud-brick restaurant that is as much a hub of Rose family life as it is a part of the business. Watching her grandchildren play around the infamous cow, Chris Rose sums it all up. "Whatever we do, we like to do it really well, so we produce wonderful wines that we are proud of. And it's so great that the business has become such a family thing. Life's pretty good." Looks like it might carry on that way too, with seven grandchildren so far, and counting.

Wairau River Wines
....
www.wairauriverwines.com
Giffords Road,
RD3, Blenheim 7273
T + 64 3 572 9800
cellardoor@
wairauriverwines.com
Owned by Phil & Chris Rose

Brand
Wairau River

Varieties Sauvignon Blanc, Gewürztraminer, Pinot Gris, Riesling, Chardonnay, Pinot Noir

Sub-region Wairau

Certified carboNZero®

Visit
11 Rapaura Road, Blenheim

• Cellar door
• Wairau River Restaurant

Taking a tip from the top

When Martyn Nicholls quit his life as a merchant banker in London to take up wine growing, he wasn't looking for a hobby. He was so serious about his new career that he went to Bordeaux to study for an MBA in wine. At his graduation, Martyn was complaining about the effects of his over indulgence in French wine and food, to which course mentor, Baroness Rothschild of Chateau Mouton Rothschild no less, retorted, "No Monsieur Nicholls, this is not fat but an image of gravitas." So Gravitas, meaning something of great stature, seriousness and elegance, became the name of the wine company that Martyn was to found in Marlborough.

Gravitas wines, which are exported to over 50 markets around the world, are made to complement gourmet foods ... and good music. A grand piano graces the tasting room and it doesn't take much to tempt Martyn to tinkle the ivories. Meanwhile, across the yard, the sharp end of the business operates out of a picturesque little cottage where we find Chris Young (above), winemaker and trumpet player. "This is a slightly crazy place," says Chris with a big smile.

Since 1995 the Gravitas team has planted 30 hectares in chardonnay, pinot noir and sauvignon blanc. "We use computer technology to manage irrigation but machines can't replace hands when it comes to leaf plucking and harvesting, so we use a lot of person-power. In the winery we whole bunch press, prefer wild yeasts, and ferment in oak barrels. We're as fussy as the French," says Martyn, who could not be more pleased with his new career, his new lifestyle and his award winning wines. Not to mention the chance to play the piano at the office.

Gravitas Wines
....

www.gravitaswines.co.nz

PO Box 23, Renwick 7243
T + 64 3 572 2731
sales@gravitaswines.co.nz

Owned by
Gravitas Limited

Brands
Gravitas, Wandering Piano

Varieties
Sauvignon Blanc, Pinot Noir,
Chardonnay

Sub-region
Southern Valleys

SWNZ accredited vineyard(s)

Visit
45 Lanark Lane, Blenheim

• Cellar door

Next year will be a doddle

When you visit the Clarks on their property at the junction of the Black Birch stream and the Awatere River, you can't help but be impressed at the pioneering spirit of Peter and Jane whose ambition to "grow something and work for ourselves" led them to this beautiful but isolated and rugged spot 12 years ago.

When they planted their first vines in 1998, their past lives, as army officer and nurse, came in handy as they struggled to learn how to be grape growers right on the edge of Marlborough's viable viticulture land. Staying calm, being organised, and dealing with the odd emergency were essential skills but they are the first to admit that they were wet behind the ears as far as their new life was concerned. "In those early days I often wondered whether we would make it," says Jane who tells of a hard bitten helper who would greet any sign of weakness with the catch-cry, "Don't worry. Next year will be a doddle." She hoped he was right.

The Clark Estate vineyard lies on two terraces where silt loam and clay form one subsoil and stony loam and sandy gravel form another, with both covering a papa sub-layer. The distinctive soil, dry, hot summers and long autumns help to develop perfect grapes, but spring frosts pose a serious risk. In one dreadful year the entire crop was lost. But the Clarks are optimists and quick to learn. They have overcome each new challenge, moving from being contract growers to producing their own wine within five short years.

Since then their efforts have been well rewarded with excellent responses to their output of sauvignon blanc, pinot gris and riesling from wine writers, award judges and of course their drinking customers in New Zealand and overseas.

Boreham Wood, named after the English town where Jane grew up and the pair were married, is a boutique label for which the whole Clark family have great ambitions. Peter and Jane's son Simon, with a degree in viticulture and oenology, has taken over the management of the vineyard and his sister Sarah, who was living the city life and working for Air New Zealand, has also joined the family business to spearhead the marketing drive.

With all the family close by, including another daughter Jennifer and four grandchildren, Peter and Jane can occasionally take a break to sit back on the verandah of their homestead, enjoying the fruits of their labours. They are happy here and with experience, the grape grower's life does get easier, but according to Peter the year when it's a doddle is something they still look forward to.

Clark Estate

www.borehamwoodwines.co.nz

PO Box 911, Blenheim 7240
T + 64 3 579 2224
info@borehamwoodwines.co.nz

Owned by Peter & Jane Clark

Brands
Boreham Wood, Clark Estate

Varieties Sauvignon Blanc, Pinot Gris, Riesling.

Sub-region Awatere

SWNZ accredited vineyard(s)

When Geoff and Diane Smith bought their first block of land in 1993 they were part of a new wave of wine growers moving into the Awatere Valley. The Awatere is now the second largest growing area in Marlborough, after the Wairau Valley, and Koura Bay vineyards are well established covering 50 hectares planted in sauvignon blanc, pinot noir, pinot gris and riesling.

Geoff, who was brought up on a farm in the Blue Duck Valley not far south of here, once worked as a fisherman. "If you come from anywhere near Kaikoura you are pretty keen on crayfish. *Kai* is the Māori word for food, and *koura* is the Māori word for crayfish. Our wines go perfectly with seafood. So there were plenty of reasons to choose the crayfish as our logo."

The vineyards, on the southern banks of the Awatere River, sit beneath Mount Tapuae o Uenuku, the highest peak in the Kaikoura Ranges. The Smiths feel very connected to this area, so much so that each Koura Bay wine is

Some local history with your sauvignon blanc?

named after a local landmark or historical event and carries a story.

All the Smiths' five children are involved in the business. Son Cameron (above) lives on the home vineyard as does daughter Kate with her husband Tim. Cameron and Tim manage the vineyard. From Cameron's cottage you can see for miles around, across the braided river valley and out west towards the ocean. The river runs close to the vineyard boundary. "If you look along the river bank you can see the soil structure that gives the grapes on the lower slopes their particular mineral character. Higher up, the soils are older clay which gives another character again."

Koura Bay wines are made by Sam Smail and the team at Whitehaven, but the winemakers can only make outstanding wines with

Each Koura Bay wine is named after a local landmark or historical event and carries a story.

outstanding grapes and that is what Cameron and Tim aim to deliver. Careful shoot thinning, hand leaf plucking, low cropping and hand harvesting are all part of the viticulture regime. "We're competitive," says Tim, "and want to keep Koura Bay on the tables of the best restaurants, so nothing is too much trouble."

"No matter what the pressure," says Geoff, "this life is very rewarding. We're working in an environment that is heaven sent and having a distinctive New Zealand product that is enjoyed throughout the world gives us all a sense of satisfaction with a job well done."

Koura Bay

....

www.kourabaywines.co.nz

PO Box 447, Blenheim 7240
T + 64 3 578 3882
info@kourabaywines.co.nz

Owned by
Geoff & Diane Smith

Brands
Koura Bay, Whalesback

Varieties
Pinot Noir, Pinot Gris, Sauvignon Blanc, Riesling

Sub-region
Awatere

A very grand plan

The numbers make your head spin as your breath is whipped away by the view across what used to be Bankhouse Station and is now the domain of Ara. 2,685 hectares of land, 1.625 million vines already planted, 1,500 hectares of vineyard to be established by 2017, the potential to supply 1.25 million cases to the market. This is wine growing on a truly massive scale.

Away to the west is the first phase of the headquarters complex built in the shape of a paper dart, custom designed to meet the needs of a 21st or even 22nd century wine business. General Manager, Dr. Damian Martin, talks about plans for Ara and another big figure trips off the tongue, "We're thinking ahead 50 years. By that time we want to be known as a sub-region in our own right, up there with the likes of Margaux in Bordeaux." Damian gained his doctorate in oenology and viticulture science from the University of Bordeaux.

Bankhouse Station was established in the 1840s and farmed by the Monro family and their descendents until 1999 when most of it was put on the market in a single lot. The broad, flat valley terrace, bounded by the Wairau and Waihopai rivers, was an extraordinary find for Auckland land developer Greg Olliver and Damian. This could be New Zealand's largest single vineyard and its consistent clay and gravel soil and micro-climate would be perfect for growing sauvignon blanc and pinot noir.

Where once award winning merino sheep grazed, grapes were soon being planted, but not before the midnight oil has been exhausted

---

Winegrowers of Ara

www.winegrowersofara.co.nz

PO Box 77,
Renwick 7243
T + 64 3 572 6020
info@winegrowersofara.co.nz

Owned by Landco

Brands
Composite, Resolute, Pathway

Varieties
Sauvignon Blanc, Pinot Noir

Sub-region
Southern Valleys

Visit
1003 State Highway 63,
Wairau Valley

• Cellar door
• Winery tours by arrangement

many times as Greg, Damian and their expert team made meticulous plans for their audacious project. "I am a great believer in traditional European viticulture techniques like high density planting to achieve low yields," says Damian, "so we want to use the best of those with the very latest technology and knowledge."

Starting from scratch, they could design the perfect vineyard, splitting it into blocks to optimise the conditions. They used steel stakes instead of treated timber posts, they built a dam, which they call Lake Pinot, and installed a water spraying system that irrigates and protects the vines from frost. Custom-built machinery was ordered, some of it robotic.

Ara means 'pathway' and a sense of determined forward movement into the future comes through strongly in everything the company is about. The Ara brand is not only a statement of origin, it is also a quality mark. The company has instituted a quality assurance system that guarantees that the wines will be the result of best

Starting from scratch they could design the perfect vineyard… They used steel stakes instead of treated timber posts, they built a dam, which they call Lake Pinot, and installed a water spraying system that irrigates and protects the vines from frost.

practice and controlled processes. Every Ara vine comes from the Ara nursery, so there is no doubt about the provenance of the grapes.

Not only is Ara producing its own wines from its vineyards, but it is also going into partnership with other winemaking companies, initially in New Zealand and eventually overseas, that want to feature a wine made from Ara grapes in their range. This is where the European model of origin brand, speaking of both location and winemaking philosophy, begins to come through and Ara's ambition to take new world wine production in a new direction starts to become a reality.

George Fistonich, owner of Villa Maria, is almost as famous as his wine label. He started the business in 1961 and is still at the helm. He is famous for believing that New Zealand wines would make it big on the world stage at a time when others were sceptical, for being amongst the first leaders of the New Zealand wine industry to understand the value of vineyard specific characteristics, and for being one of the first to move totally to screw caps. He's famous for being a very astute businessman and for dishing out down to earth business advice, like "If you want to be a success, concentrate on the people."

Villa Maria's Marlborough people are led by another George, George Geris, (below, right) "Yes I do occasionally get mistaken for the man himself," says George G with a wry smile. Before becoming the winemaker here over 10 years ago, George backed up his post graduate qualification in viticulture and oenology with experience of winemaking in South Africa and Australia as well as some of the less well known wine regions in Italy, Hungary and Greece where his father's family came from.

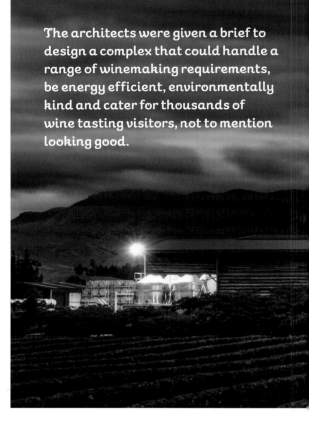

The architects were given a brief to design a complex that could handle a range of winemaking requirements, be energy efficient, environmentally kind and cater for thousands of wine tasting visitors, not to mention looking good.

World-wide reputation for getting it right

Not long after George arrived at Villa Maria he was asked the question every winemaker would love to hear, "What do you want your new winery to be like?" It was a once in a lifetime opportunity, to work with the architects to design a state-of-the-art facility that would become the all purpose hub for the company's operations in Marlborough. The architects, Archemedia, were given a brief to design a complex that could handle a range of winemaking requirements, be energy efficient, environmentally kind and cater for thousands of wine tasting visitors, not to mention looking good. The resulting design, a series of superimposed horizontal layers in steel and cedar, compliments the flatness of the river valley and the backdrop of the local hills. The Marlborough Villa Maria crew like their home

which has weathered well and settled comfortably amongst the vines.

Today, George Geris and viticulturist Mike Croad (far left) are concentrating on pinot noir. Villa Maria has been a leader in securing Marlborough's reputation for sauvignon blanc which continues to be the label's leading Marlborough variety. But George believes that pinot noir is the region's other big story. "It's not an easy one to perfect, but we have the climate for it and its pretty stable so we can be confident about what we're getting. I've been delighted with the pinot we've been producing and our buyers are just loving it."

More than four decades after winning prizes for his first wines at the 1962 Royal Easter Show, George Fistonich's taste for business, for innovation and for keeping Villa Maria at the forefront of the New Zealand wine industry, is as keen as ever. Were he alive today, George's father, an immigrant from Croatia, would be proud and possibly surprised to see what has come from leasing his son a two hectare slice of his small Auckland vineyard all those years ago.

Villa Maria Estate

www.villamaria.co.nz

Corner Paynters &
New Renwick Roads, RD2,
Fairhall, Blenheim 7272
T + 64 3 520 8470
enquiries@villamaria.co.nz

Owned by Fistonich Family

Brand Villa Maria

Varieties
Sauvignon Blanc, Riesling,
Pinot Gris, Chardonnay,
Pinot Noir, Viognier

Sub-regions
Wairau, Awatere

SWNZ accredited vineyard(s)
SWNZ accredited winery

Visit
Corner of Paynters
& New Renwick Roads,
Fairhall, Blenheim

• Cellar door
• Winery tours by arrangement

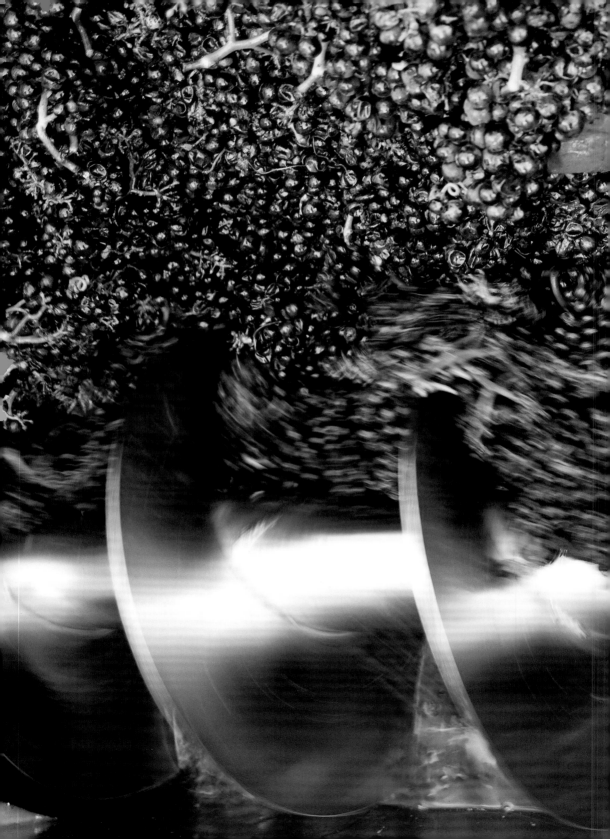

Marlborough Wine Celebrations

February is the ideal time to enjoy a celebration in Marlborough. Summer is at its peak, the vines are well on the way to delivering another vintage and it is time to have some fun. Since 1983, February has been the time to celebrate Marlborough wine and food at the Marlborough Wine Festival.

Visitors travel by air, sea, rail and road from throughout the country to enjoy the weekend and overseas visitors to New Zealand organise their itineraries to make sure they catch this special festival. There are welcoming events on Friday and on Sunday the region's restaurants put on their best show. There are also boat trips on the river or in the Marlborough Sounds – with food and wine of course. But the main event takes place on Saturday, amongst the vines of the Brancott Valley, when over 55 wine companies and around 25 food producers present their wares for festival-goers to sample whilst being entertained by the country's finest performers.

In odd numbered years, Wine Marlborough organises a second weekend of celebration – The Marlborough Wine Weekend. Less of a party and more of a homage to Marlborough wine, the weekend offers a programme of wine tastings and superb wine-matched food prepared by local and guest chefs.

The weekend happens in October, around the time that many of the new vintage wines are released. It attracts wine and food enthusiasts, from novice to expert, who enjoy the variety and fun of the programme, the excitement of sampling new wines and adventurous cuisine and the pleasure of sharing all this with like-minded company.

Marlborough Wine Festival – 2nd weekend in February every year. www.wine-marlborough-festival.co.nz
Marlborough Wine Weekend – October every 2nd year. www.wine-marlborough.co.nz

The Wine Exhibition

When you walk into the
The Wine Exhibition
at Marlborough Museum
in Blenheim, you are taken
back to the days of the early
Marlborough wine pioneers
such as David Herd. The
exhibition looks back to the
earliest known grape growing
and wine making enterprises
and tracks the evolution of
Marlborough's wine industry
from the 1870s through to the
present time.

Perhaps the first thing
to catch the eye is the huge
collection of iconic, old, rare
and unusual wines displayed
along with modern examples.
Quite apart from their contents,
the bottles themselves are
fascinating – so many different
shapes and sizes.

The viticulture and
winemaking equipment on
display ranges from basic
to sophisticated and amongst the tools and
machinery there are some ingenious technological
inventions rescued from sheds around the region.
The founders of Marlborough's wine industry were
nothing if not inventive.

Photographs and other personal
memorabilia tell the story of the people involved
in making Marlborough what it is today and
describe the social changes that have happened
over the decades.

As well as displays of artefacts,
audio-visual and interactive exhibits bring to
life the history of Marlborough wine and make
The Wine Exhibition a must see for visitors to
Marlborough, whether wine lovers or simply lovers
of a great story of Kiwi ingenuity.

The Wine Exhibition will be a permanent feature of the
Marlborough Museum from February 2009.

26 Arthur Baker Place, Blenheim

T + 64 3 578 1712

info@marlboroughmuseum.org.nz

www.marlboroughmuseum.org.nz

Listings

Tours
. . . .

deVine Tours Marlborough
T 0800 devine (338 463)
info@devinetoursmarlborough.co.nz
www.devinetoursmarlborough.co.nz

Join us for the inside story of Marlborough wine. Tailor made tours, strolling in the vines, visiting wineries and enjoying amazing views with a knowledgeable guide. All based around a gourmet lunch and wine tastings. *All year.*

Explore Marlborough Personal Tours
T + 64 3 579 5765
info@exploremarlborough.co.nz
www.exploremarlborough.co.nz

Personalised tours showcasing the best of Marlborough. Wine tours by bike, food tours and half day walks. *All year.*

Highlight Wine Tours
18 Buick Street, Blenheim
T + 64 3 577 9046, highlight.tours@xtra.co.nz
www.highlight-tours.co.nz

Enjoy a full or half day wine tasting amongst Marlborough's finest wineries, with lunch option available. We are flexible with start and finish times and offer you your choice of wineries to visit. *All year.*

Marlborough American Limousine
18 Buick Street, Blenheim
T + 64 21 854 129
info@americanlimousine.co.nz
www.americanlimousine.co.nz

Experience the wineries of Marlborough in the comfort of our Super Stretched Lincoln Limousine. Seats 8–10 and air conditioned for your comfort. Full or half day tours. Your choice of wineries and restaurants to visit. *All year.*

Marlborough Sounds Shuttles & Tours
16A Admiralty Place, Waikawa, Picton
T + 64 3 573 7122, + 64 21 133 5946.
drive@marlboroughsoundsshuttles.co.nz

Chauffeur driven tours – wine, boutique food producers, arts and crafts, scenic and gardens. Door to door shuttle service. *24 hours a day, 7 days a week.*

Marlborough Travel Greenshell Mussel Cruise
T + 64 3 577 9997, info@marlboroughtravel.co.nz
www.marlboroughtravel.co.nz

Cruise the stunning Marlborough Sounds to a Greenshell mussel farm where you will taste the freshest steamed mussels matched to a glass of Marlborough Sauvignon Blanc. What better way to experience this wonderful region. *November to March.*

Marlborough Travel Wine Tour
T + 64 3 577 9997, info@marlboroughtravel.co.nz
www.marlboroughtravel.co.nz

Experience the fabulous Marlborough wine region on a half day or full day guided tour. Join a group or let us tailor a wine or full gourmet tour just for you. *All year.*

Na Clachan Wine Tours
T + 64 3 578 8881, + 64 21 171 4861
helen@naclachan.co.nz
www.naclachan.co.nz

Relaxed, friendly, flexible tours around Marlborough's finest wineries. Your knowledgeable guide is a contract grower for a local winery. *All year.*

Sounds Connection
10 London Quay, Picton
T + 64 3 573 8843
tours@soundsconnection.co.nz
www.soundsconnection.co.nz

A variety of daily scheduled tours around the Marlborough wine region. Private charter and group options available. Also boat charters. *All year.*

Restaurants
. . . .

The Chartroom Restaurant
The Yacht Club Hotel
25 Waikawa Road, Picton
T + 64 3 573 7002, info@theyachtclub.co.nz
www.theyachtclub.co.nz

Enjoy mouth-watering, European-influenced, Kiwiana dishes and accompanying Marlborough wines in our award-winning, maritime-inspired restaurant. *Open all year.*

Drylands Restaurant at Drylands Winery
237 Hammerichs Road, Rapaura, Blenheim
T + 64 3 570 5671, restaurant@drylands.co.nz
www.drylands.co.nz

Our restaurant team serves superb seasonal menus to match the pick of wines from Drylands, Rose Tree Cottage, Nobilo and Selaks vineyards. Indoor and outdoor dining. *Open Wednesday to Sunday for lunch and Thursday, Friday and Saturday for dinner.*

Gibb's Vineyard Restaurant
258 Jacksons Road, Blenheim
T + 64 3 572 8048, info@gibbs-restaurant.co.nz
www.gibbs-restaurant.co.nz

Enjoy exceptional cuisine, outstanding wines, and excellent service with a smile. Vineyard dining with European flair using seasonal produce. Dinner for two, dinner with friends, a special celebration or business – you'll have a memorable experience.
Open for dinner November to April 7 nights and May to October Tuesday to Saturday.

Gusto
33 High Street, Picton
T + 64 3 573 7171

Exceptional food. Great service. Freshly made counter and menu selection including vegetarian dishes. Brilliant coffee, relaxed atmosphere, local wines and beers.
December to April open for breakfast and lunch 7 days and for dinner on 5 nights Tuesday to Saturday. May to November open for breakfast and lunch, closed Saturdays.

Herzog Restaurant at Herzog Winery
81 Jeffries Road, Blenheim
T + 64 3 572 8770, info@herzog.co.nz
www.herzog.co.nz

Enjoy fine European cuisine prepared by Michelin star-rated chefs in our luxurious award-winning restaurant. Indulge yourself with our famous 5 course Degustation Menu matched with Herzog handcrafted wines, or lunch in the bistro. *Open mid October to mid May.*

Highfield Restaurant at Highfield Winery
Brookby Road, Blenheim
T + 64 3 572 9244, restaurant@highfield.co.nz
www.highfield.co.nz

With sensational views from Brookby Ridge, Highfield specialises in New Zealand and Mediterranean inspired cuisine, focusing on fresh local produce. Indoor and outdoor dining. *Open daily for lunches.*

Hunter's Garden Café at Hunter's Winery
Rapaura Road, Blenheim
T + 64 3 572 8803, restaurant@hunters.co.nz
www.hunters.co.nz

Enjoy café-style dining and sample Hunter's wines, in the garden, under the verandah, or on cooler days, in front of the fire.
Open daily for light meals and lunches except Christmas Day, New Years Day and Good Friday.

Kaikoura Winery Cliff Top Café
140 SH1, 2kms south of Kaikoura
T + 64 3 319 7966, info@kaikourawinery.co.nz
www.kaikourawinery.co.nz

With stunning mountain and ocean views, the Cliff Top café is the perfect place to enjoy our all day menu and Kaikoura wines.
Open 10am to 5.30pm all year (later in summer).

La Veranda at Domaine Georges Michel
56 Vintage Lane, Rapaura, Blenheim
T + 64 3 572 9177, frenchtoastltd@gmail.com
www.georgesmichel.co.nz

Come and relax in tranquil surroundings. Enjoy delicious, rustic vineyard fare and fine Marlborough wines, for brunch, lunch and functions. *Open all year. Tuesday to Sunday.*

Le Café
Waterfront, Picton
T + 64 3 573 5588, lecafepicton@xtra.co.nz
www.lecafepicton.co.nz

Transparent cuisine. Locally landed Fish and Seafood, NZ wine, Havana coffee, Cuban cigars, Live Music, Local art, Home-baked goodies. Stunning View!
Open daily from 7am until late.

Lochmara Lodge Café
Lochmara Bay, Queen Charlotte Sound
T + 64 3 573 4554
enquiries@lochmaralodge.co.nz
www.lochmaralodge.co.nz

Relax in our fully licensed café/restaurant with stunning bay views. The seasonal menus offer simple, rustic options epitomising the flavours of Marlborough. We specialise in local, wild and organic produce with a focus on seafood.
Open mid September to mid June.

Montana Brancott Winery Restaurant
State Highway 1, Riverlands, Blenheim
T + 64 3 577 5776, information@montana.co.nz
www.montana.co.nz

Our restaurant is the ideal place to take a break from your exploration of Marlborough's wine country. Enjoy our varied menu for a late breakfast, lunch or afternoon tea.
Open all year. Closed public holidays.

Saint Clair Estate Cellar Door Café

Corner Selmes & Rapaura Roads, Blenheim
T + 64 3 570 5280, cellardoor@saintclair.co.nz
www.saintclair.co.nz

A delightful vineyard café serving fresh
seasonal food matched with wonderful wines.
Enjoy a friendly, relaxed environment for tasting
and dining.
Open 7 days from 9am to 5pm.

Twelve Trees Restaurant at Allan Scott Winery

Jacksons Road, Blenheim
T + 64 3 572 7123
twelvetrees@allanscott.co.nz
www.allanscott.com

A popular lunchtime venue with a great menu
featuring Marlborough produce. Dine in the
leafy courtyard with its fountains and topiary,
or in winter the cosy interior and open fire
provide a warm welcome.
Open all year for lunches.

Wairau River Restaurant

on Wairau River Estate
T + 64 3 572 9800
restaurant@wairauriverwines.com
www.wairauriverwines.com

Our restaurant, with its wide verandahs and
stunning views is a perfect place to relax
and enjoy lunch and Wairau River wines. Our
menu features local produce prepared fresh
every day.
*Open every day for lunch except for Christmas
Day, Boxing Day and Good Friday.*

Dining at Waterfall Bay by Seresin Estate

T + 64 3 572 9408, jan@seresin.co.nz
www.seresin.co.nz

Nestled amongst native bush in the
Marlborough Sounds, a simple timber cabin
converted into an intimate dining room.
Degustation dinners feature Seresin wine and
food from some of the best chefs from around
the world. *See website for dates.*

Whitehaven Restaurant

1 Dodson Street, Blenheim, T + 64 3 577 8166
whitehavenreservations@xtra.co.nz
www.whitehaven.co.nz

Relax and unwind in our secluded cottage
garden restaurant and enjoy our varied menu
of fine food and Whitehaven wine.
Open all year for lunches and dinners.

Accommodation

171 on High Motel

171 High Street, Blenheim
T + 64 3 579 5098, info@171onhighmotel.co.nz
www.171onhighmotel.co.nz

Stay in style. Twelve modern, stylish units.
Warm, friendly southern hospitality. 5 minute
walk to cafés, restaurants, shops, conference
centre. *Open all year.*

AAA Marlin Motel

33 Devon Street, Picton
0800 100 784, rest@marlinmotel.com
www.aaamarlinmotel.com

Come rest in spacious accommodation,
relaxing indoors and in your garden, complete
with grapevines, citrus and native trees,
encouraging tuis into your tranquillity. Full
kitchens, bathrooms, TV, etc. Easy convenient
parking. *Open all year.*

Antria Boutique Lodge

276 Old Renwick Road, Blenheim
T + 64 3 579 2191, stay@antria.co.nz
www.antria.co.nz

Antipodes meets Mediterranean, stunningly
different architecture with cool covered
verandahs. Original New Zealand art
throughout. Luxury bedrooms with huge
ensuites will ensure the best night's sleep in
quiet surroundings. Gourmet breakfast and
complimentary local wines. *Open all year.*

Bay of Many Coves Resort & Spa

Bay of Many Coves, Marlborough Sounds
T + 64 3 579 9771
enquiries@bayofmanycovesresort.co.nz
www.bayofmanycovesresort.co.nz

An elegant New Zealand retreat, set in the
heart of the Marlborough Sounds. Tucked away
on the shores of a stunning aqua-blue bay, this
is the perfect contemporary haven to enjoy
peace and quiet in comfort and style.
Open all year.

The Bell Tower on Dog Point

Brookby Road, Blenheim
T + 64 3 572 8831, info@thebelltower.co.nz
www.thebelltower.co.nz

Situated in Dog Point Vineyard, on a hillside
amongst the vines overlooking Marlborough's
beautiful Wairau and Omaka valleys. The
Bell Tower on Dog Point offers luxury B&B
accommodation. *Open all year.*

Brancott Ridge Bed & Breakfast

226 Wrekin Road, Blenheim
T + 64 3 572 9140, stay@brancottridge.co.nz
www.brancottridge.co.nz

Exclusive luxury bed and breakfast
accommodation in an elevated and secluded
location. The two guest suites have views of
mountains and vineyards. Elegantly furnished,
fully air conditioned and includes guest lounge,
swimming pool and gardens.
Open all year except July and August.

Brydan on Rose Motor Lodge

Corner Middle Renwick Road & Rose Street,
Blenheim
T + 64 3 578 4312, stay@brydan.co.nz
www.brydan.co.nz

16 spacious suites and apartments (Qualmark
5 star) set amongst extensive grounds with
heated swimming pool. All units have superking
beds. *Open all year.*

Chardonnay Lodge

T + 64 3 570 5194,
info@chardonnaylodge.co.nz
www.chardonnaylodge.co.nz

Bed & breakfast and self-contained villas in
landscaped, park-like grounds, swimming pool,
spa pool and tennis court. *Open all year.*

Chateau Marlborough

Corner High & Henry Streets, Blenheim
T + 64 3 578 0064
chateau@marlboroughnz.co.nz

www.marlboroughnz.co.nz

Marlborough's 5 star luxury boutique
accommodation in the heart of Blenheim.
Enjoy an environment of seclusion and comfort
with attentive yet unobtrusive service. New
luxury suites, boardrooms, café dining, bar and
heated swimming pool. *Open all year.*

Driftwood Beach Bed & Breakfast

226 Rarangi Road, Rarangi
T + 64 3 570 5007
info@driftwoodbeach.co.nz
www.driftwoodbeach.co.nz

We are situated right on Rarangi Beach, Cloudy
Bay. Stunning views over the Marlborough
Sounds, Pacific Ocean and Wither Hills.
Open all year.

Escape to Picton Boutique Hotel

33 Wellington Street, Picton
T + 64 3 573 5573
bookings@escapetopicton.com
www.escapetopicton.com

Escape offers luxury accommodation,
restaurant and wine bar, situated in the heart of
the picturesque town of Picton. Luxurious stays
do not come any better than at Escape. Picton
is the gateway to the Marlborough Sounds.
*1 September to 30 April, 7 days. May to August
limited hours.*

Framingham Cottage

Conders Bend Road, Renwick
T + 64 3 572 8884, info@framingham.co.nz

Bordering a picturesque stream, this charming,
self-contained, 3 bedroom cottage is on the
Framingham Estate. Bookings essential.
Available all year.

Isabel Lodge on Isabel Estate

Hawkesbury Road, Renwick
T + 64 3 572 8300, info@isabelestate.com
www.isabelestate.com

Fully self-contained lodge situated within
our vineyard. Spacious, cozy, with open log
fireplace. Suitable for couples or groups.
Available all year.

Jasmine Court Travellers' Inn

78 Wellington Street, Picton
T + 64 3 573 7110, info@jasminecourt.co.nz
www.jasminecourt.co.nz

Quality accommodation in the heart of Picton.
Quiet, comfortable, self-contained motel
studios for the discerning traveller. 5 star
Qualmark rated. Close to departure for Queen
Charlotte Track, Marlborough Sounds and
Wellington ferry. *Open all year.*

Lochmara Lodge Wildlife Recovery and Arts Centre

Lochmara Bay, Queen Charlotte Sound
T + 64 3 573 4554
enquiries@lochmaralodge.co.nz
www.lochmaralodge.co.nz

Relaxing nature retreat amidst native bush on
the shores of the Marlborough Sounds. 14
rooms with stunning views and access to
Queen Charlotte Track, Marlborough Sounds
and wine region. *Open mid September to mid June.*

Accommodation continues on next page >

Listings

Accommodation continued

Lugano Motor Lodge
91 High Street, Blenheim
T + 64 3 577 8808
luganomotorlodge@xtra.co.nz
www.lugano.co.nz

High quality 4 star plus accommodation in central Blenheim overlooking the lovely Seymour Gardens. Two minutes walk to cafés, restaurants and shops. *Open all year.*

Marlborough Vintners Hotel
190 Rapaura Road, Renwick
T + 64 3 572 5094, info@mvh.co.nz
www.mvh.co.nz

5 star accommodation set amongst the vines and the blossoming cherry trees, adjacent to our restaurant and bar. A perfect location on Rapaura's golden mile of world class wineries. *Open all year.*

Olde Mill House B&B & Cycle Hire
9 Wilson Street, Renwick
T + 64 3 572 8458, 0800 653 262
info@oldemillhouse.co.nz
www.oldemillhouse.co.nz

Stay in Renwick, the heart of the wine region. Over 25 cellar doors within 5kms radius. Three top class rooms all with ensuites, set in beautiful gardens. Complimentary cycles, spa, barbeque, wireless internet. *Open all year.*

Old St Marys Convent
776 Rapaura Road, Blenheim
T + 64 3 570 5700, retreat@convent.co.nz
www.convent.co.nz

One of New Zealand's finest country retreats, situated on an estate of 60 acres of vineyards and parkland. Luxurious guest rooms with claw foot baths and separate shower. Swimming pool, petanque, croquet, bicycles, billiard room. *Open all year.*

Palm Haven Bed & Breakfast
15a Otago St, Picton
T + 64 3 573 5644, palmhaven@xtra.co.nz
www.palmhaven.co.nz

A modern, well-designed, purpose-built B & B on the Picton hills overlooking Mt. Freeth. 5 min walk to the waterfront. Continental breakfast. Complimentary fruit bowl, glass of Malborough wine and transfers within Picton. *Open all year.*

The Peppertree Luxury Accommodation
3284 State Highway 1, Riverlands, Blenheim
T + 64 3 520 9200, info@thepeppertree.co.nz
www.thepeppertree.co.nz

A luxurious and beautiful restored Edwardian villa, built in 1901. Set amongst beautiful gardens, own boutique vineyard and olive grove. Five individually decorated guest suites ensure you enjoy your stay in privacy and comfort. *Open all year.*

Straw Lodge Boutique Vineyard Accommodation
T + 64 3 572 9767, strawlodge@xtra.co.nz
www.strawlodge.co.nz

Straw Lodge provides stylish 5 star accommodation. Guests occupy private vineyard suites and enjoy wonderful views, complimentary tasting of the vineyard's wine, use of bikes, spa, golf clubs. Meal options plus self-catering available. *Open all year.*

Stump Creek Lodge
21 Stump Creek Road, Blenheim
T + 64 3 570 2090
reservations@stumpcreeklodge.co.nz
www.stumpcreeklodge.co.nz

Idyllic private setting, superb vista through vineyards, free pick-up from ferry and airport. Self-contained, pool, spa, barbeque. Continental breakfast. *Open all year.*

Tamar Vineyard self-contained Cottage
67 Rapaura Road, Rapaura, Blenheim
T + 64 3 572 8408, tamar.vineyard@xtra.co.nz
www.tamarvineyard.co.nz

Situated in the heart of the wine trail, our self-contained vineyard cottage is a warm romantic retreat, with a fourposter bed for your comfort. Our breakfasts are legendary! We look forward to welcoming you. *Available all year.*

Timara Lodge
Dog Point Road, Blenheim
T + 64 3 572 8276, timaralodge@xtra.co.nz
www.timara.co.nz

Timara Lodge is one of the country's most luxurious and private lodges, hosted by its own internationally renowned and Michelin-experienced chef. Timara Lodge promises an unforgettable experience and a haven of peace, quiet and relaxation. *Open September to June.*

Vintners Retreat Resort
55 Rapaura Road, Blenheim
T + 64 3 572 7420, info@vintnersretreat.co.nz
www.vintnersretreat.co.nz

Villas Amongst The Vines. 14 serviced, self-contained, luxury, spacious and private Villas accommodating 1–6 guests. Pool and tennis court. *Open all year.*

The Yacht Club Hotel, Picton
25 Waikawa Road, Picton
T + 64 3 573 7002, info@theyachtclub.co.nz
www.theyachtclub.co.nz

We offer the perfect haven from which to explore picturesque Picton, the enchanting Marlborough Sounds and the Marlborough wine region. *Open all year.*

Art Galleries

Art Studio at Hunter's Winery
603 Rapaura Road, Blenheim
T + 64 3 572 8489
www.hunters.co.nz

Artist in residence Clarry Neame welcomes guests to view his work which includes pointillism, landscapes, portraits and abstracts. He works with brush and palette knife. *Open daily 9.30am to 4.30pm.*

The Diversion Art Gallery
at Grove Mill Winery
Corner State Highway 63
& Waihopai Valley Road
T + 64 274 408 121
info@thediversiongallery.co.nz
www.thediversiongallery.co.nz

The stylish tasting room hosts a programme of exhibitions by some of New Zealand's most collectable contemporary artists including paintings, drawings, sculpture and limited edition prints. *Open 7 days – cellar door hours.*

Oriel Gallery
35 High Street, Picton
T + 64 3 573 5353, info@orielgallery.co.nz
www.orielgallery.co.nz

Contemporary art by emerging and more established artists from throughout New Zealand including paintings, sculpture, jewellery, ceramics, glass and more. *Open daily in summer, reduced hours in winter.*

Oriel Sculpture at Seresin Estate
Bedford Road, Renwick
T + 64 3 573 5353 , info@orielgallery.co.nz
www.orielgallery.co.nz

An exhibition of sculpture by New Zealand artists, set along the upper terrace of the home vineyard, near the cellar door. *Open cellar door hours.*

Lochmara Lodge Wildlife Recovery and Arts Centre
Lochmara Bay, Queen Charlotte Sound
T + 64 3 573 4554
enquiries@lochmaralodge.co.nz
www.lochmaralodge.co.nz

See art in a different space. Visit the outdoor sculpture trail amidst native bush. Two indoor exhibitions and concert galleries. Artist in residence studio. Residential workshops. The Centre is also home to EcoArtists New Zealand. *Open mid September to mid June.*

Millennium Art Gallery
Corner of Seymour & Alfred Streets, Blenheim
T + 64 3 579 2001
marlpublicart@xtra.co.nz
www.marlboroughart.org.nz

Marlborough's public art gallery presents a high quality, varied programme of nationally touring and locally developed exhibitions and events. *Open 10.30am to 4.30pm weekdays, 1pm to 4pm at weekends. Closed some public holidays.*

Gardens

Hunter's Native Garden at Hunter's Winery
603 Rapaura Road, Blenheim
T + 64 3 572 8489, wine@hunters.co.nz
www.hunters.co.nz

Our native garden features many trees, shrubs and grasses typical of the dry plains of Marlborough's Wairau Valley. A new addition to the garden is an area dedicated to rare and endangered Marlborough plant species. *Open daily except Christmas Day, New Years Day and Good Friday.*

Wine & Food Events

Blues Brews & BBQs	*February*
www.bluesbrews.co.nz	
Marlborough Wine Festival	*February*
www.wine-marlborough-festival.co.nz	
Havelock Mussel Festival	*March*
www.musselfestival.havelocknz.com	
Forrest Estate Grape Ride	*April*
www.graperide.co.nz	
Saint Clair Vineyard Half Marathon	*May*
www.vineyardhalf.com	
Pinot at Cloudy Bay	*June*
www.cloudybay.co.nz	
Silver Secateurs competition	*July or August*
www.wine-marlborough.co.nz	
Young Viticulturist competition	*July or August*
www.wine-marlborough.co.nz	
Marlborough Sounds Festival	*September-October*
www.marlboroughsoundsfestival.co.nz	
Kaikoura Seafest	*October*
www.kaikoura.co.nz/seafest	
Marlborough Wine Weekend	*October 2009, 2011*
www.wine-marlborough.co.nz	
Marlborough Farmers' Market	*October to May every Sunday morning*
www.mfm.co.nz	
Hunter's Garden Marlborough	*November*
www.garden-marlborough.com	
Marlborough Agriculture & Produce Show	*November*
www.marlborough4fun.co.nz	

Further Information

Book orders

Wine Marlborough
T +64 3 577 9299
admin@wine-marlborough.co.nz
www.wine-marlborough.co.nz

Visitor Information

Destination Marlborough
T +64 3 577 5523
info@destinationmarlborough.com
www.destinationmarlborough.com

Picton i-Site Visitor Centre
The Foreshore, Picton
T +64 3 520 3113, picton@i-Site.org

Blenheim i-Site Visitor Centre
Blenheim Railway Station, SH1, Blenheim.
T +64 3 577 8080, blenheim@i-Site.org

Wine Industry Information

Wine Marlborough
T +64 3 577 9299
admin@wine-marlborough.co.nz
www.wine-marlborough.co.nz

Sustainable Winegrowing New Zealand
T +64 3 577 2379, sally@swnz.org.nz
www.nzwine.com/swnz

BioGro New Zealand
Organic certification agency
T +64 4 810 9741, info@biogro.co.nz
www.biogro.co.nz

Marlborough Information

Marlborough District Council
T +64 3 520 7400
mdc@marlborough.govt.nz
www.marlborough.govt.nz

Index of wine companies

Wine words

Biodynamic
A method of organic agriculture introduced in 1924 by the Austrian scientist Dr. Rudolf Steiner.

Cellar Door
A tasting room where wines can be sampled and purchased.

Méthode Traditionelle
Sparkling wine made in the traditional Champagne method.

Oenology
The academic study of winemaking.

Organic
Growing in harmony with nature without the use of chemical fertilizers or pest controls.

Release
The release of new vintage wine onto the market.

Terroir
A French word, pronounced *ter-wah*, most commonly used in New Zealand to mean the unique combination of soil, topography and climate found in any particular place.

Variety/varietal
A botanical variety of grapevine.

Vintage
The year a wine was made. Also used to refer to the annual harvest and winemaking season.

Viticulture
The science and art of growing grapes for making wine.

Winemaking
The science and art of making wine from grapes.

Abbreviations

BioGro – BioGro New Zealand Inc. – an organisation that sets standards for organic growing and production of food and accredits organisations that meet those standards.

SWNZ – Sustainable Winegrowing New Zealand – an organisation that sets good practice standards for sustainable growing and production in the wine industry and accredits those vineyards and wineries that meet those standards.